Another Way

Another Way

Living to live again

Supernatural Soldier

Order this book online at www.trafford.com
or email orders@trafford.com

Most Trafford titles are also available at major online book retailers.

Printed in the United States of America.

ISBN: 978-1-4269-5981-3 (sc)
ISBN: 978-1-4269-5980-6 (hc)
ISBN: 978-1-4269-5979-0 (e)

Library of Congress Control Number: 2011903899

Trafford rev. 03/16/2011

 www.trafford.com

North America & International
toll-free: 1 888 232 4444 (USA & Canada)
phone: 250 383 6864 ♦ fax: 812 355 4082

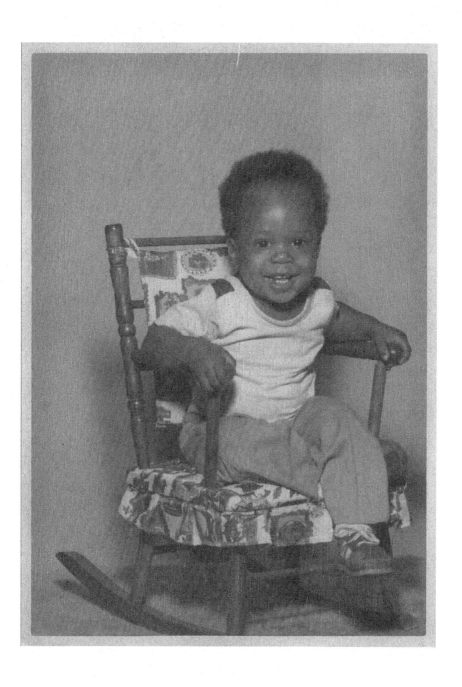

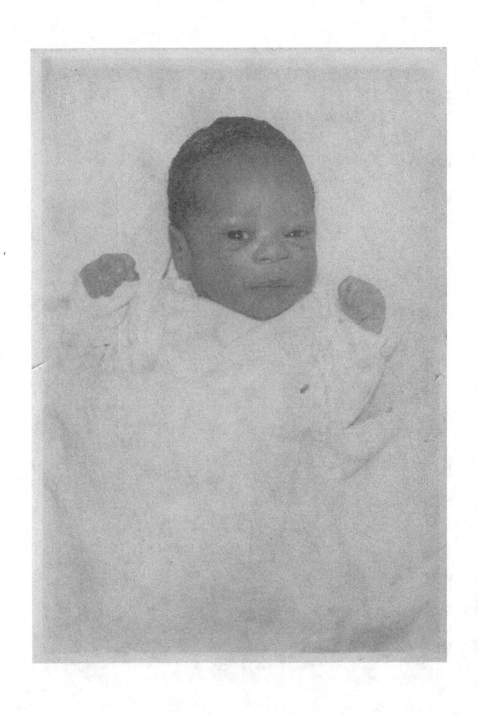

"Dedicated to my aunt pam who died durinng my 90 days in jail I know she would be proud of me"

"This pic is very significant because it symbolizes that my dad hadn't left us in the projects yet to go to Indianapolis to start a new family teh beginning"

I would like to give honor to my Mom for the great job she did by the grace of God raising five children on her own in the inner-city of MI. I dedicate this book to all those inexperienced parents who aren't perfect by no means and are doing the best they can by their natural ability. Dear Mom I am at a point in my life in comparison to Moses' and the relationship he shared with his mother. The blessing of forgiveness starts within the individual I ask God to help me with this process daily just as you did for your children. My suffering through mental pain and anguish was a direct result of inexperiences of the unlearned. I love you and may the peace of God rest rule and abide in our hearts now and forever Amen!

The pivotal point in my life before my first daughter was born and before the part-time job at Burger-King. I was headed to the state track meet that year 93-94 my Junior year of High School. I was a functioning alcoholic, marijuana abuser during all of my days in H.S. nothing to be proud of or change. My sufferings in those days were self-medicated by booze, fighting at home with my stepdad and anger. I was able to stay focused in school because the books gave me a escape away from my reality. As my writing may reflect my parents were strict but they told me I could be all that I could before I knew how to spell or say army and I believed them. You know what they never told me that my attraction would be altered by the wrong way of living watching people I look up to party hard and live an irresponsible lifestyle. Nevertheless I wouldn't change a thing because my past is what is shaping my future by grace and mercy.

Dear Dad a little overdue to express my feelings after over twenty plus years thanks for opening my life to a happy display of family. I actually was able to have the best of both worlds aside from all the abuse and pain and pressure on this side of the family tree. Although there was never the sign of neglect the pain from child abuse was ever present and that is why today. I have a story to help those who suffer the abuse another way to channel the anger that corrupts the mind body and soul of a traumatized young man women boy and girl. I am proud today to give honor to a pass life that was filled with ups and down happy and sad times good old fashion experience. I guess I know what I'm talking about now I love Indianapolis and the blood covering of Jesus to keep us through the test and trial of life. If it had not been for the Lord on our side you wouldn't have taught us how a family structure was supposed to look. Oh how great we as children had it especially me. I had two sets of parents in two different states trying to get it right by the grace of God. We all fall down and get back up I heard a powerful influence in my life lately say Set Backs are setups to come back with King Jesus. The chastisement keeps me out of prison today for that I am thankful peace

Here in America it is tradition to make the unknown history we have wonders of the world and great Spiritual wonders. Here on earth my family tree is a wonder deeply rooted in my soul "Where I Come From" my dad genealogy of children. We were joined together by the forces of divine inspiration to overcome all the obstacles great or small in God's eyes the weigh the same. Rico I love you and could never imagine the heartfelt trauma you struggle with even to this day about being stripped of your rights to decide who you'd rather live with regardless of the nature of character of a person inexperienced in raising children. Little sister's remember when we had a family talk and dad thought it useful for me to address the life I lived in MI. the safety of a older brother for his sister's was placed in my heart and I am here to let you know that irresponsibility flows from leader to follower. Our parents did the best with less than we have available today and under the kinds of pressure they faced in our younger years. We should just be thankful we always had heat water a roof and hot water to bath with Amen. Our strife to the top doesn't suppose to be good feeling all the time or we wouldn't learn.

Love Temple
Church of God in Christ
PO Box 831 Henderson, KY 42420

February 24, 2011

Greetings,

    This letter is being written in reference to Brother Willie Pringle, pastoral assistant and member of Love Temple. As Pastor of Love Temple, in 2008, I became acquainted with Bro. Pringle thru fellowship with another colleague in Morganfield. In 2009, I was informed of his move of residence to Henderson in which he resided at the Harbor House and needed a place to worship. Bro. Pringle began to fellowship and later joined the Love Temple ministries in which I began to mentor and assist in his transition. Thru this assistant he achieved employment, housing and began to development in character.

    As I mentored Bro. Pringle, his qualities of humility, intellect, honesty, as well as a diligent spirit evolved even more. He has moved on to conquer and overcome the many failures and setbacks in his life. Those setbacks of alcoholism, broken relationships with his children, family and God have begun to heal and have allowed growth in many other areas. He is fulfilling his goal of higher education, raising his children admirably and maintaining a covenant relationship with God. He has now achieved another plateau in his life and that is the dream of his theatrical production that is now a reality. As Pastor, mentor and friend, I wish Bro. Pringle all the success life can bring him!

Committed to Christ,

Harlan C. Armstead Sr.

Supt. Harlan C. Armstead, Sr.
Pastor

Preface

The book *Another-Way* was written by Willie Pringle. It is the beginning of my new way of living safe and sober. The entire new path is divinely designed by the grace and mercy of God and it keeps me encouraged to help people in society do the right thing. I can't begin to express how happy I am to be able to tell my story of how God blessed me to overcome the abuse of alcoholism. Thinking back to how many brushes with death God has brought me through to this very day, I know that I am blessed to be living. I have purpose in life to share my experiences, strength, and hope with those people still suffering.

I used to live a life of a binge drinker. Some people relate to this as a weekend or a day when they were hung over from a party. I am from the streets of Michigan inner-city, where the liquor stores are open on Sunday. Things that I was doing to my body when I was abusing alcohol will only affect my body, but I couldn't learn that small lesson. The booze had my reality blinded by the desire to always stay drunk, 24/7 p.

The first thing I had to subconsciously do was surrender my will to God and basically get out of the way. I had to surrender to putting myself through the humiliation of character defects that came along with alcohol abuse. The first chapter of my walk with God started in January 2008, when I was describing the sin of my alcoholism. The sin of alcoholism to me means my slow spiritual death certificate. I wasn't willing to accept that I had a drinking problem. I was strong enough to get drunk every day. I was super-sick in my sins where reality was watered down. I was losing weight on alcohol like I was on heroin or worse. My desire to drink was active daily, with no resting at all.

I have been sober three years now and I am still battling the attitude "spend it until it is all gone." With every issue I was the innocent one and those closest to me were at fault. I wasn't going to allow anyone to tell me anything to make me feel any different about drinking. I felt that when in Rome act as roman. The co-dependent side of me was always around those friends who boosted my ego. I didn't have my own identity. I'm not a crack-head. Alcohol is liquid crack to me. I use to stand on the block pointing at crack heads but I wasn't any better when I was doing petty hustling to get more drinks. You know, sticks and stones will break your bones, and drugs and alcohol will break the rest. I am so grateful that I am sober. Before I got sober I was in a state of sickness.

Chapter-1

I have empathy for people who are still suffering through abuse of addiction. I used to be just like those people. In my first steps toward a new beginning and a new way of living I had to surrender. I had to admit I was the problem and that drinking and partying made things in my life worse. All of my life I was used to doing what I was only big enough to do. I thought that the way I was raised was the only way. I tried to live up to those expectations and embarked on powerlessness. I am not totally against my old way of life because, believe it or not, I did have fun. The fun was in the beginning when I thought it was smooth to be drinking like a grown-up at a young age.

This is for parental advisory because I didn't achieve sobriety by doing the right thing. My life story unfolds in general from the time I can remember until present. I must start with the chemical history — not to embarrass anyone — but to allow the details of the story to take shape. I want to leave a lasting image on the minds of the readers that all things are possible if we believe. The second time I was in counseling at the same treatment center I was told to complete a time line. On my time line I had to note any changes — increase or decreases — in my drug and alcohol usage. I had to note the times that I may have tried to stop using drugs or drinking. I had to note times that I went to treatment, or suffered from any major positives or negatives.

I was told there is no right or wrong way to answer, so I was to be creative, be thorough, and be honest. The survey asked the first age I ever took a drink of alcohol. At the age of seven I had a cup of gin at the spur of the moment. There was no positives at the time. I was too young at the time to know that was a negative. My stepdad knew better than to give it to me. I used to drink out of beer cans any time the family would have parties. Those were positives, I thought at the time. I believed I would grow up to be better at drinking and partying than my relatives. The negatives were that by getting away with sipping all the time my drinking tolerance grew as I grew. By age 8 I was sipping gin and beer like a half a half. Every time I thought about my sister and brother molesting me I would drink more, even as a child. The positive was that I was so young but in my gut I knew it was wrong. The negatives were morally disgusting.

I was introduced to these obscene ways of life in the household I was raised in not outside. Nevertheless I am really stressing the point that as a child I was able to hold all this inside and hide it. I didn't have any outside influences to harm me. All of my abuse came from the immediate family. The positive moments I had as a child included playing in the projects I grew up in called Berrien Homes. When I was in the projects, which was comprised of two streets shaped like a U, I was in paradise. The negatives I had were confusion, hurt and shame. When I turned ten I quit using. The molesting stopped and the negatives were my attitude was unusual (not like that of a ten or eleven year old). I started thinking about my situations and still couldn't confront my sister and brother about how I felt about them molesting me.

As my life took a turn for the worse at the age of seventeen I felt close to the edge. At the same time I felt like I was on top of my responsibility. But I was a coward. I was a co-dependent to booze and the in-crowd. I didn't sit still long enough to recognize my problem. I was unmanageable and wouldn't allow anyone to manage or mentor my life into correction. I was told to delve into my trauma and find peace from all stress. I was thirteen years old and my habits were back — marijuana and drinking. I had a high tolerance for marijuana, a pint alcohol, and many beers a day. I never partied alone. I always had a few friends with me every day, all day.

I enjoyed sharing with my friends. We were all crazy. I loved getting a buzz and enjoyed the wild life from fourteen until thirty one years of age. At 19, I graduated from high-school and I was drunk at the time. I joined the Army that same summer. I was rebellious. What on earth made me join the army? Looking for a free ride? I saw money, not the work involved. By the age of 19 I was drinking beer like apple juice and had a high tolerance for marijuana. I lived to get buzzed up. My life at this point was a binge living experience. I was drunk awake or asleep. If I ran out I would sell other drugs to get more drinks.

I was what they call a petty dope seller. I didn't sell to make a extra dollar. It was women and drinking for me. I was a first-time dad by the time I graduated from high school. I got married to my baby mom because I thought it was the right thing to do. I was trying to do better than my parents. My parents never married because of the same reason I shouldn't have. We were too young. My marriage didn't change the issues we were facing in the relationship. I was drinking even more and neglected my responsibilities. I had every excuse for neglect: The wind was blowing, the children were asleep, the water running, for example. I guess from the ages of 21-23 I knew in my heart I needed to do better. I didn't know how to do it. I thought I was too tough to stop on my own I needed God to literally show up in the flesh and prove to me he was real.

Mark my words I started to recognize things even being drunk. I was heavy drinking during this time. I am not trying to offend any married people. I am not opposed to marriage. It is honorable in the sight of God, but not when two teen-agers are manipulating the roles of husband and wife. I wasn't a good leader by example of a good husband or dad. I didn't have any examples in my home. I ran from my issues and I had a plan toward a future that I wasn't trying to share with family. My wife and I were cheating on each other before the marriage. The marriage lasted for fifteen years. We were happy for the first eight months living on base in Fort Knox.

I admit I enjoyed that relationship. There were no rules or guidelines. We made them up as we grew apart. Nevertheless, things took a turn for the worse. Both my alcohol abuse and the domestic abuse increased. I have already served my debt to society for this. At the time my mentality was almost ruined. I was a player until my baby mom started bringing her boyfriends to the house. I'm not justifying anything because I used to have girls pick me up in front of the house. I changed after I came home one morning about 5:30 am. I came into the house, and I couldn't hear a peep. As I walked through the house to the bathroom my wife was on the couch. A guy I went to school with was buttoning up his shirt in our bathroom. It didn't surprise me but I was hurt, and I meant to leave without a fight. As was leaving, my wife asked me for some money for a bill.

You mean to tell me you hate me that much? You can't cheat and get paid to do it. After that there were numerous times, but the last straw was her stripping on the coffee table in front of my children. I am telling you this because for every action there is a reaction. I had a nervous breakdown. When all this stuff was occurring I couldn't take it any more. I was outside the window. As I looked through the window I could see the backs of my daughter's heads as they watched. I saw it all. I gathered what was left of my composure as best as I could and went into the house. I was hostile burning with rage, but in my heart I was crying "God please help me." I wasn't going to shoot anyone with the twelve gauge I had gotten from my grandpa Johnnie's house. I did get my point across. My baby mom told everyone to stay, that they didn't have to leave. I snapped because of all the love that was lost after that moment. I lost it and I gave up on the world.

I was at a house party when the nervous breakdown started to show. The party was for senior citizens. My friend's mom was having her birthday party, and the majority were older than 60. We were smoking and drinking. I was really catering to everyone being nice and missed the rolling of the marijuana. I had my own and I should have just let them go ahead. I didn't want to be left out. Someone put medicine in the marijuana. I was already hyper enough without marijuana. I hit the joint a few times and had my beers. I should have been smooth but my heart was racing. I couldn't sit still. I was ready to get rowdy, the more and more I sat around doing nothing. I felt like yelling so we began to freestyle and all of a sudden I was outside. People were telling me to calm down. I was screaming at the top of my lungs. I didn't care.

My friends took me home and left me. The next three months were an episode to remember. The party had been in September 1997. By February 1998, I had been to the psych ward for a week. I was tripping. I was having fun. I was playing with some children in the neighborhood. We were playing with pancake mix. To this day those children remember that I was willing to go the extra mile to keep them happy. The episode was serious. I know God got my attention in that psych ward. My dad was supposed to be this powerful minister all my life and my mom speaking in tongues and testimony. I saw and heard them pray for other people but when this was going on with me they were powerless. I came to them both and they didn't know how to handle that demon I was dealing with at all. Mom put up with it for about three months then told my dad to come and get me. Only twenty four hours convinced him I was in need of psychiatric help.

I was really upset with them, but my dad always left me in time of trouble except when the punishments were being issued. I got abused by them whipping me so much with leather dog leashes and extension cords. I had to wait until I got older to voice my opinion about the trauma from the beatings I feel were worse than a slave master to his slaves. At least then I understand the connection. While I was in the psych ward I had time to realize what God was doing with me. I had to stop putting myself through the humiliation I saw other people suffering. People who didn't even know their own names. I witnessed people limp on beds like vegetables in gloom. I had become a ward patient. I let go of my grip on life. I loved people more than myself. This may sound all bundled up but the abuse was there on all sides.

I was raised in the projects of Michigan in the inner city, which is no excuse, in a small three-bedroom apartment in the inner city of Michigan.

My mom and dad both have five children. I am in the middle on my mom's side and the second oldest on my dad's. I didn't get along with my stepdad because we were both alcoholic. I saw my oldest sister and brother fight with him so much when I got older that I thought it was the thing to do. I was bashed with verbal abuse all the time. My stepdad would say that my dad never wanted me. My stepdad never talked tough when my dad was around. After my episode with the marijuana back in 1997-1998 I never picked it back up. I blamed it on the marijuana like D-Bow in the movie Friday. It had me in the chicken coop. My alcoholism went sky high. I drank more in those last years of my drinking than I ever had. I am truly blessed to be alive. I was still ignoring my children and my wife. I am blessed I didn't catch anything or get seriously hurt by one of those fatal attractions.

This is just a preface to what the book really unfolds. During 97-98 I received a domestic violence on my baby mom. We play too much and she had enough and tried to take me out. One morning I was awaken with her on my chest. I was under all the covers and she had me. I couldn't even scream, "Baby I love you." She had the knife on my neck and had that look in her eyes. I had so much running through my head, but I really didn't want to say a word. I knew the sound of my voice would get me stabbed. Play time was over, and I didn't have any jokes. One thing about our relationship was that when I got nervous, I would crack jokes that were not appropriate for the time. This was one of those times, so I chose my words very wisely.

I said, "I know you don't want to be left to explain to our children why you killed their dad." I felt her pause, then I said clearly, "I know it hurts. Our relationship isn't all that, but it's not worth spending your life in prison thinking about it." When she glanced at the clock, I flipped her over. I was in my boxer shorts looking for my clothes, but she had them hid. The boiling water was already ready when we tumbled down the stairs like a sack of potatoes. My baby mom grabbed the water and chased me back upstairs. I jumped in the shower and turned all the cold water on. When she threw that pot of steaming hot water at me I screamed like a lady in the delivery room. The nosy next-door neighbor called the police. The neighbors thought all the screaming was my baby mom, but it was me. I knew I was going to jail when I saw the lady cop. My baby mom put on the best acting Golden Globe performance. I saw her crying she can't take this anymore. I was the one bleeding from the gash in my arm. I had knots on my head and tried to show the police the redness from the hot water.

When I was put in the police car the police were laughing at the story. The police officer took my work money out of my pocket without checking my check stub and gave it to my baby mom. I was misused that day. I prayed that this material will produce a book that will help people to see that if I made it through all my problems. I know they can make it through. God has a plan for everyone.

Now I am moving into my move from Michigan to Kentucky in December 2006. Upon my arrival to the surrendering to sober living I had to go to jail for 90 days, which was the longest time I had ever been in jail at one time without getting out for good time or bail. I got out of jail with the mind trying to work it out, but of course history repeating itself. I had two DUI's in one year and my license suspended for 18 months. The only thing about it is I was going to the alcohol and drug treatment program free willed. I wasn't forced. I knew I had a problem. I have grown accustomed to accepting hardship as a way of living in a relationships. I did it to myself and I needed help to see what could be done about it. I went back to the ex-girlfriend because I wanted to know the truth. Instantly I learned on November 20, 2007, (my out date) that I was just a friend. I lived with her until April 1, 2008, realizing that two people can't walk together except when they agree.

I was headed toward living sober and she thought nothing was wrong with having a drink. We were like oil and water, no mixture. I was tired of living spiritually dead. As I started to write out my pain and the emotions I had in the beginning of my sobriety, I was scared I didn't know how to live without drinking and abuse. I didn't really know what to expect or what I wanted out of this life. I didn't want my attitude and animosity to be my death. People were always telling me they saw me in a greater light. Then I could see myself throughout my life. I was carefully listening for how to become better. I was waiting on the promises of God, though at first I wanted God to work instantly.

I didn't realize that it had taken almost half a life time for me to get this way. I was the opposite of every positive thing people who didn't drink were used to. I wasn't considerate of feelings I wasn't accountable I didn't cherish things like nature. Now I look at the world as God's house. I try to view everyone as guests in God's house to be treated with Godly love and consideration. I am merely a servant in God's house. I must be ready to do all I can for those who still suffer and need help. There is gladness in God's service. There is much satisfaction in serving the most High God. I am saved so others may be saved and sober so that others may be sober. My walk with God is not for me to keep to myself. I have to share with all the living. While we are living in our Father's house I am grateful for the victories.

I have so much gratitude in service work for God's children. By helping others God continues to help me. I pray that my work may be a small repayment for God's grace so freely given to me. I was asked a question about the sin of drinking. The deeds done to the body on earth shall pass. My body is the temple but my soul is the spirit. The heart and mind make up the soul. The disaster of drinking in my life was a death certificate to me. Everything was over exaggerated I was sick and needed God's help to be delivered. I lost weight on alcohol like any other addict. When I quit drinking the most important lesson I learned is that now I had to deal with character. I needed to pray or read my bible or take a scripture to work to stay routine. I tried to stay focused on fixing me. I got into quarrels with myself and other nonsense.

I acted as if no one understood me. I thought I could change the world and I can't. Note: Be careful not to try and change the world. If you see things that need to be changed look in the mirror. I feel that I don't have time to worry about other things that are wrong. I am not perfect. In the beginning I would be obsessed with something. My mind and body felt like I had been on a drinking spree without the bottle. I was alcohol free but the signs and symptoms were the same. My thinking follows a pattern of "it's my way or the highway." Everyone and everything is either with me or totally against me.

This is step one. I am typing it from old papers so keep that in mind. Lately thoughts have been occurring to me, and when I use my patience and things I've come to learn from being a new person I don't immediately act like I use to. I think about what could happen and the bottom line to the outcome of things. I'm still working on my attitude in this area. I have acted on conversations lately and just daily activity with the ex-girlfriend. I got all hay-wire then thought "oops I handled that wrong." I have to consider people's feelings first. If my actions affect people in a disturbing way I have to think before I act. I was compulsively anxious and wanting to have pity-parties, but not on purpose.

I thought that once I was finally sober I would get some respect from people who always wanted me to be sober. I had the wrong idea. It wasn't right and it was short lived. I got a quick understanding of the two-way street and the grass is green on the other side. Then I would flash back to years ago and get depressed about that old stuff. They didn't even use to know I was tripping. They didn't even know fifteen years ago what the problem was. It didn't even involve them.

Physically I'm too skinny to lose weight. I lost eight pounds drinking nothing but alcohol, mentally telling myself I'm the best when I felt worthless. On the inside I was spiritually out of touch with God the Father of my Lord and Savior. It seemed like my conversation with God was echoes of my worthless drunken breath. I received two DUI's in one year and four days and before that I had just gotten my license back. Emotionally I was a sip and a accident away from set-back or death. I feel like it's okay to cry. But I didn't. All I had to do was cry out to God before the drama hit. Alcohol numbed my face and filled my head and heart full of concrete. I was a knucklehead.

Recently I have still found myself yelling constantly and repeating myself, trying to do too much instead of slowing down my patience and calming my nerves. I haven't been getting enough sleep. Third shift is killing me but my attitude has been off the hook. I have been obsessed with a problem with problems come problems. My relationship with my girl at the time was upside down and she didn't understand fully what her role was yet. Now that I've quit drinking it's new for her so I got to understand. We had to readjust. I had to believe more and have faith I got it. I need to stop allowing negativity to cloud me and my time. I keep having drawbacks meaning I'll get two steps ahead of my recovery and in a calm place of serenity, all to mercifully understand that I'm a piece of dirt scum and that God created me to be just as He was in an image.

I haven't adjusted to the new me cause I get beside myself every now and then. I am more aware of these behaviors that are better forming so now as I'm trying to recover without the alcohol. I can handle situations openly and positive. I was in denial about drinking so much that I use to say I wasn't an alcoholic and could stop anytime. As I got into the littlest argument with my girlfriend or family I had an excuse to get drunk. I changed the type of alcohol I drank to lite beer thinking of it as an excuse to drink because I wouldn't be affected like usual. I planned my drinking from pay check to pay check trying to drink the liquor store out of business. The drinking was at the top of the list of demands before pay day. Soon as I had money in my pocket, drinking was involved until the last penny was spent. I was innocent and nothing could tell me or make me feel any different.

No one understood my drunken point of view. When in Rome act as Romans. When around my social group it just made me want to drink more. I'm not a crack head and never did anything harder than weed laced and it didn't kill me. I'm not a crack head. Alcohol is legal liquid crack to me. I use to stand on the corner. I thought I was doing good, at least better then a crack head drunk. My buzz off alcohol was just as high as a crack head. Matter of fact I did things. I did things just like a crack head to get drunk. I stole and sold drugs and myself like a fluke. Just remember when you point one finger three pointing back at you. Stick and stones break bones and drugs and alcohol will break the rest. Yes before I got clean I was filthy sick and tired and still sick and tired.

Every day was Halloween. I prayed to God that I would live to see the Sunrise. I want my legacy to live on for all those people who have lost their loved ones to suffering. Let me slow down. We all got a grave. I want to die peacefully with so much peace and alcohol and drug free. I pray to behave. I want to live longer. Plus my children are getting much bigger and soon to be young adult women. I want to be remembered as gentlemen. I don't want my last memories to be isolated and cold. I want to give them wisdom. I am embarking on life. My path is already paved. I was a monster and did what I wanted regardless of the consequences. Right or wrong it is a part of life so I'm doing my best. that's all God wants.

I understand no one expected me to achieve. I understand sometimes I expect myself to fold at the point of no return. There's not enough information on living life without stress and alcohol. I can't do it alone. I pray for unity in the community and learning new things daily. I just ask God to open my mind to enhance my ability to learn more and more. I don't want to violate any laws. A law abiding citizen isn't for show. I can do all things through Christ. Those that won't allow God to steer the wheel won't make it. I got to get a transformation like Saul to Paul. This is just the first step toward recovery.

When I was in my alcoholism I was scared to face reality. I was blinded by the truth that I was losing out on the good side of myself and attitude. I always owned up to my acts of silliness. It's a shame that it took so long to see how foolish I was and had become. This is my life. At first I couldn't think past life without alcohol. Now I can see clearly and the alcohol and drug free clean life I lead. I don't even get illegal cable. I'm good. I want this to really sink into the mindset of free people, free kingdom, free world free agents. This life is greater. Big dreams and big expectations are fulfilled out of good behavior. Results are like the bricks the Egyptians made for each pyramid. The impact they had on society is big. The point is people will talk about you doing good or bad. You can't avoid them but don't join them. Just think it's a lot of great people striving and great people suffering. All I know is that I am a child of God.

Chapter 2

I use to claim all sorts of things but this is the most powerful. When I realized all the time I had wasted it hit me hard. Always free loading. I was worthless. Always broke. I couldn't pay attention. I was always acting up like that favorite clown. Isolation took over. I began to drink and drive heavily plus small jail visits brought me to recovery. The ninety days in Morganfield county jail on wanton endangerment and fourth degree assault second DUI in a year. The situation that formally led me to work on myself and leave alcohol alone was tragic.

As I was serving ninety days in jail (the longest jail time I ever served during thirty-one years on earth), I was in confinement for the longest time ever. I was still in denial at first. I was full of animosity cause it was everyone else fault I was locked. Once I got comfortable being in jail my Aunt Pam died. Her funeral was in Oct 2007. Even her death helped me realize I needed help to quit drinking before it was my funeral. I recognized my alcoholism was a major problem when my girlfriend kept making excuses to see other dudes. I didn't come to Kentucky from Michigan for all of this. Anyway we would argue, and she would leave me at the house by myself and the booze. I didn't have a license so she left frequently, the entire time cheating on me with people I hung with.

Now this one night I turned into the hulk. We were arguing as usual with nothing different but what was going on in my mind. Between the sip of cheap Gin and Milwaukee Best I thought I was going to. I saw it all in my mind. Once she got in the truck I was going to get on the bumper. In my mind it made sense, but I didn't actually think I would make it. My girlfriend grabbed her purse and keys and cigarettes and stomped out the house. I jumped on the back of the Expedition during the ride I examined my life. Let's see I drink gin and beer. I only smoke cigarettes. When I drink I wasn't a cartoon super hero I was scared. Here we are speeding down the street in Morganfield, KY with me on the back. I was trying to talk to her. Every time she heard my voice she punched the gas. I climbed around the side of the truck.

Once I got to the front of the truck we fought. I got in the truck to stop it. I was crazy. I apologized whether she accepted or not. Remember it's my recovery. The actions and reactions always start with self. I've got to get it right starting by admitting. I'm admitting I used to be an alcoholic. Forget anyone else. But in jail I wrote her a book. Then God worked on me. He put on my mind that no one can help me get to the kingdom of heaven but me. So with that we can pray and help each other all day. Some will understand and some won't. I tried until I was blue in the face to fix things until I finally stopped to fix myself and work on myself. I was no good to anyone else then. I wasn't even court ordered to do counseling. During my ninety days I almost went to a treatment center as I thought about treatment. I didn't need treatment to start drinking I don't need treatment to stop. I involved meetings and church and new friends in my life. I even went to the extended program at the counseling sessions.

I had done a six month program that was supposed to be ninety days the year before. I guess I am a knucklehead. The short program wasn't for me. I needed the intense counseling. Now that I've come back to the beginning this is where my problem should've been corrected. If that counselor hadn't put our business in the newspaper when I was molested I would be cool. Now is the time because I've always had excuses to drink and been in situations that were life threatening, and still drank sooner or later. Now sick and tired of being sick is why I decided to get my life together. I have to overcome powerlessness as a stepping stone to a new beginning.

When I was down and out I couldn't call on nobody but God. Powerlessness over alcohol really had a hold on me. The things I've done fought my ex's and baby-mom in front of my children. The cheating during the marriage on both of our parts was useless. I was a petty hustler selling drugs to get drunk, a bum jeopardizing my freedom and sanity. I had to place reality before pride and fix the problems I face with good intensions. Arguing over things I have no control over know way. But I will not subject myself to put up with non-sense if it makes my attitude act up.

I've manipulated my alcoholism by stealing from other people lying all the time to myself and others. I was a very disrespectful to myself, and females as to using them for pleasure sexually. I'm evil more disruptive could careless attitude mean tempered aggressive protecting myself is by all means necessary. Manipulative very felt that I could con a nun out of some sex. If she gave me a few seconds I manipulated people to maintain my addiction yes bribe people for money or whatever. Made up stuff to get drunk I quit everyday just always wanted to cause I could I guess. No I quit on my own cause

I know it's either dead or in jail and I'm not good at serving time in jail lack of freedom. Actually sense I've quit my life has improved dramatically I wish I would have did it sooner.

I can see the sunny days and the shining sunrise in the end now all I got to do is focus on getting stronger. I need strength to fight this fight on God's side sober-minded and clean. I found out that it's twice as hard to be clean and sober the protection is more powerful and precious. My children barely see me we each suffer differently but we still love I can't get those ninety days back three months of my life gone. I was full of stress and depressed to be so far from my family. Locked up over a girl who didn't even tell my family I was locked up. I've kept up with my career of drinking in 20-25 years yes I've been arrested in Michigan no DUI. I only had an OUI now two DUI's in a year Morganfield was a gift and a curse. At thirty-one years old I remember the public intoxication in Indianapolis at twenty-seven.

I was getting my CDL's about to take the driving test but a friend thought it would be good for me. If I would swallow his bag of buster weed no one was buying it all day. Plenty of things I have done and been around I wasn't caught selling dope knock-on wood. I made a little penny huh stayed at the mall drinking and messing with females. I was hustling on and off hanging around family and friends that sold drugs. If we'd got caught the time offered would start after 20 years. God is wonderful to have protected me. At work not so much back then as trouble I was out there. So gone over alcohol if I went to punch a clock at first it was to double the money from the check every week then it became a habit of walking off the jobs just say forget it and leave. Once I was so drunk at work in Indianapolis that my crew had to cover for me.

I was wasted I needed a stone cold whipping. When I was in high school no trouble cause it was either don't go, skip, or go, and then leave during school to go get messed-up. My sisters didn't like me drinking they used to love hanging around me. Not when I was drinking they hated my guts. My mom she tolerated me but always reminded me of how my step dad died from alcohol poisoning. So I should want to stop never worked until I wanted to stop. I had trouble with friends who cared if they were true friends we are still friends. Now if those so called friends are upset. Oh well let them be haters true friends don't let friends drive drunken. We all did man God was with us all those times I made it to the driveway waking up in the car like how we make it home. My way doesn't quite cut the mustard. Even if my way is not talking to other people outside of our relationship about our problem's making our problem more than alcohol.

First you were upset because I drink too much. Now you're talking about me while drinking and smoking with dudes who clearly want to see us in turmoil. My anticipation on being the one who needs to communicate in our relationship was off. I found out that if just leads to more fights so skip it insistent patches don't work well not any of mine. I consider people feelings all the time. I try to I was clouded by acts of pity I hype self-up to think I'm considerate. At times but drunk I have no consideration it's have you considered what you'd do to me. Yelling or people swearing they hate you for me when I was drunk those words make me feel great.

Now I'm like a good Dave Chappelle episode is that it. Alcohol is ignorant-oil to me. I've took drastic measures all the time but they'd crash not overwhelmed is soft for me I was moody I needed a drink doing everything. I didn't understand the alcohol-free life I was so gone thinking about me off alcohol what is it after that man I got my motivation back. I can't fall apart I'm too focused plus alcohol is a drug. I can't twist the lug nuts I need a beer man the children they rude I need a beer or I been drinking I'll argue until day break and go get drunk again.

People use to say man you won the effect is like oh-Willie hide the drink. Huh oh-Willie's at it children. My crisis mentally is just when we argue about how many sheets of tissue do I wipe my bottom. It was this moment when I remembered how I use to behave fighting, in bars, gangs. Once I hit the panic button it was on I can't go back to jail someone said it wasn't prison. It wasn't supposed to be either I am no good at being treated like a criminal if so I'd be retired and rich back then. My health has been bothering me I got this little pain in my thigh. But haven't worried t much kind of slow on that I haven't saw my children in like three years and it hurts but not like it use to I would pass out drunk or call they house even though they mom would curse me out. Oh well just said bless her I'm still praying once my divorce is settled I'll have closure.

When in danger I was dating this old head with six children she was old enough to know better how she was acting. Still messing with ex-I was drunk off Belvedere and she let him in the house I was passed out he could've killed me. If I would've been in my right mind I would never have been involved with her or her situation. I have harmed plenty of people as a result of my alcoholism. But there's nothing justifying my behavior this I know during my rampage. Only for a second I enjoyed causing harm to those who offended me. My baby mom cheated on me with different dudes. I already knew how to cope with that kind of hatred. I didn't know what compassion was like there's plain anger or in-crowd pressure. We as in the gang use to control our hood.

As if the law was failing we'd make other fiends buy from only our group muscle. We never went against the grain we hurt people in a major way of governing the activities associated with gang violence. Nevertheless to say it back fired eventually we each all fought amongst each other. Crazy an out of control these day's I am very talkative and argumentative working on it. I have temper tantrums I call them anxiety attacks. Things don't go my way I'm ecstatic very paranoid yelling at people my girl getting nervous and calls people to tell on me. No one can get words in edge-wise Losing it and cursing only makes the problem worse I use to feel trapped misused and hen-picked. It's all fun and games until somebody get smacked in the mouth. Violence is not the answer. I smoked weed because I thought it calmed my nerves.

Everyone I knew said weed helps but they were the main people going through it and wouldn't accept mentoring. Any substance that alters the mind or thought process is a bad thing. Weed helps my mind is too smart for all that I am to intelligent for the devil to take me away that way. I thought I knew it all listening to knuckleheads acting just like me none of my friends were trying to live right. All weed did was boost my anger I don't know what it was it ignited my fire. Then I was never without a drink alcohol's the drug of choice throwing fuel on the fire. My insides were lava

I became so angry nothing started to change. I pushed and things started to push back until I couldn't punch anything at all not even a thought through my mind. I mean I was depressed a mess my feelings got worse.

I created a red-zone of exile the red-zone took over my reality as long as I tried to store up a web of get angry later space. My thoughts and pressure wore me down like Jason and Michael Myers. I was slowly going in rewind dying more and more day in day out. I have accepted my measurement of the alcoholism simply put all measurements and volumes of drugs sold and alcohol drank during my trip was enough. Most of the people I've associated with respect me because I don't go around them anymore. My family that still used the ones I know I can't go around and stand firm. They can't even ride on my handle-bars of my bike. I'm comfortable in some surroundings where I used to get drunk because they do it meaning I got to know what alcohol did and does to me. So I can't ridicule anyone else for their use. No that's Russian Roulette having drugs around eventually I'd be selling getting fast money.

The old behaviors had to change wouldn't connect I'd be drunk before the next thirty minutes. Crazy selling dope to get drunk my character was like a dope fiend junkie. God said all things old become new I had to surrender my will to God. God's will be done anything's possible through God the Father of my Lord and Savior. I thank God for allowing his Son to be the Savior he knew we would need a Savior. I believe in Jesus like I use to believe in those fifths and beers getting me drunk the spiritual high is the greatest. I wake up with energy no hang over I know every second God has forgiven all my sins. As long as I pray and keep the line open from my heart to his I will be great. I can't imagine any problem being to devastating that I have to be afraid.

The word is God and God sent Jesus who became the word to survive the hurt first. So we wouldn't have to suppress or suffer yes my spirituality my faith my belief in God my closeness, my comfort-zone, my burden bearer, my rock, my salvation, My reservations being caught up Jesus I am headed to the promised land. I want everlasting life I am going to trust in God with all my heart. So when all the saints start marching I want to lead the band or song. When God comes back I want to be ready I want him to remember my service work.

First of all the police yelling your surrounded Willie get down on the ground in August 20, 2007. I realized there was something about the dirt in KY and dust sinking into my fresh clothes getting dirty in Morganfield, KY. Listening to the girlfriend yell I hate you I hate you leave me alone. I got an open mind and my road to this point was hell to pay. I went through hell already and God forgave me. Now it's time to do my best the positive best. I've done mischievous things to long why did I hurt myself so much. Why was I comfortable with people hating me I was ready for some relief. I felt like a fugitive finally caught after a twenty-five year escape I was spiritually tired of running. I needed stability the thought of incarceration see some people know some people. Since I wasn't raised in Kentucky none of the people in jail was from my hood. I didn't know nobody I was cold inside God was right there for me.

Now I got day to day things that go along with my routine jail isn't one of them. God keeps me in check as long as I ask for his help he guides my ability I have to have blind faith. I must stay out of self and more in tune with God the way he wants me to be as patient nice human being. I am to be like inspiration not frustrations, inspire everything good and bad things. Personally to completely surrender you have to exterminate the entire problem all of it not missing one inch of area cause the bug's will still be there. You can begin I just do not think without a surrender it will be best cause you are leaving yourself open for destruction.

My life is like I'm strong enough to deliver stand up the plate backing down from nothing because whatever turmoil was created during the use was wickedness. Now that God is taking care of all that I can rest I can smile I can think clear I am strong I can and I will not I can't I'm afraid or those but, if's, can't, won't doubt, these are no longer my attitude I got strength I got power good thoughts and great demeanor. Eventually things blow-up look at trying to avoid surrendering like this someone right now somewhere is going through worse. Somebody is tricking to get higher or selling drugs to children under twelve to get re-up.

People in the neighborhood are eating out the garbage cans. Many children are sleeping in allies starving. Someone somewhere right now is dropping dope off to elementary teachers to serve children. There is children somewhere 10-12 hooked on drugs and pills and heroin. There's teenagers being raped at home an in prison's man fighting the no winning Battle to surrender only makes things worse. If you love drama then go head I don't I can't I won't I surrender every day I die daily through God's will. I got a safety net God has the answers to my problems I pray them to God he is a healer my all he watches over me. Now all I've been thinking about doing it the next right thing. All of three years one month and six days I've dreamed of drinking once with my dad no reality I never wanted him to see me doing any wrong. The reality of my alcoholism is I'm striving for sobriety.

I did all the damage no matter how long I stay clean I've done the damage and got to live with certain ailments. Plus the fact that one is not enough and a thousand isn't either. Nevertheless I have fastened my mind towards God and purchased prayers from heaven with my pray card. Thanking God for my Lord and Savior Jesus who is heading the bright and dark times and conditions in my life. I have been subject to remember things people think to personal not to me I'll tell it get it off my chest Lying creates confusion liars are conniving so they think. Well I use to get asked by ones that knew me. Where you been where you going when you coming back they use the three second rule on me now. If I answer in three second s or answer all the survey they'll know that I'm telling the truth thinking my people in other states didn't actually know I was a alcoholic.

Please I can tell them a few good old stories maybe they already know but they maybe now know I'm on a better plateau. I heard stories of other reservations I'm having trouble believing this cause you are what you eat. You make your own destiny. I've heard answers to the reservations and they were silly. God has all the reservations you need I am practicing open-mindedness. By not taking advice toward me as insults like I use to I'm looking forward in regards to being free from pain and suffering. So I must call-up God and reserve some strength and faith courage and any positives. Plus allow him to tear down all the evil I've created and rebuild things inside as well as outside my well being. So I can live happy strong enough to handle things once they appear no more running.

I am willing to follow some sound advice from mentors and community sponsors. I know I am one who needs constant direction yes I have been following directions tremendously. I have been going to church and a few meetings without having or being court ordered. I thank God I did complete al the counseling sessions it took for me to get here. I have the privilege of admitting that I am at the top of the bottom know where to go or turn but up. My family and friends are not involved in this transformation I gained. A considerable amount of self respect with sobriety God has all power may you find him now or be doomed to repeat history. I am willing to give living life sober all I have and more.

Let's see in all my getting I shall get a understanding about life and consequences. My best efforts is paying close attention to my perspective accept advice willfully gain positive manners to replace any negatives. I must work a process that takes careful compassion. Accept another way as my new path of life. Hurdle over all my brick walls like Olympic medalists. Keep the faith in God and last but not least be inspirational no one can deny the power of God. I don't care not even the devil can resist the Power of God. I have freedom. I was Rick James and didn't care who knew that's how I felt during my alcoholism. I use to party all the time drinking mainly because I wanted it was my soul purpose.

Even when people worlds were in turmoil I was still drinking day or night happy or sad. I drink so much until I forgot exactly what was I doing it for. I was rarely hurt and if I was hurting I never felt it until somebody else explained how they may have tapped out cause of 9-11 or death's in families. Oh not Willie I was hype everyone got thrilled or laugh's off seeing me act a fool they could easily ignore. Whatever problems they had my actions were example enough. My sense of relative importance I have always been crafty. Always been 3.579 GPA. Nevertheless I can assume my position as a grown up finally standing firm and dusting my shoulders off. I needed a pick me down or kick in the hand-me downs to get up and get it all finalized. I want peace I want greatness and positive effort.

This may take time and skill but all I got is time and skill. I got my health strength and encouragement from family and friends. I am finally accepted in every position I'm living positive in society. Oh I'm not the enemy any more the British aren't coming now the Gov isn't at fault for supplying the world drugs and taxing can't use drugs or sell it. The government can put it in coke cola. Inject soldiers with LSD like lab rats and do nothing okay. I'm sober now those things aren't of any of my control so I pray God handle me. Give me the strength when I and where I am weak. Quench my thirst for the truth church. I use to be a alcoholic stealing from people to get drunk. I sold drugs for a drug crazy things I use to hold dope in my socks on the block waiting for fiends stings.

I had the nerve to call myself a drinker crazy thinking I was better. I was Rick James all kinds of nick-names it's hip to be square just Willie. Hi my name is Willie I am a grateful saved sober free peaceful living citizen. I am on the higher rise rising higher and higher on this level. I can't allow no one and nothing to come between my freedom and my sobriety even if family and friends.

I have to lose to be saved and sober I feel the spiritual gift of sensational relief. I've accepted so much in my days but accepting the fact that I am dealing with alcoholism and that God erases all my sins. All things are made new white as snow I'm a precious gift that merciful scripture of Dust and breath from God above. I have joined church and know it's time to move on to a bigger city. I've learned all ready to stand firm in my research and sobriety. This is the first step toward a new life for the rest of my life.

My bottom came first this step is last I wish I could've done last first this is a new beginning. A new beginning to a world as I've never knew it free and sober my prior knowledge has actually helped in some way's but nothing changes the pain or cuts to the chase that one day one inch one step one second one millimeter at a time is all we can afford to work on cause nothing is promised yesterday is gone tomorrow has yet to come. So today all day I must ask God to lead me guide my attitude help me give me strength to get away from who spitefully abuse me. I thank God for waking me up spiritually mentally and physically. Thank you for taking me through all the drama and trauma in my childhood. I pray that you have mercy and forgive those who molested me and beat me over the limit.

Most of all God, I thank you for carrying me through all those obstacles. I still needed more beatings I was just your son trying to learn from people who didn't have a clue. I got that from a lot of rules 2-DUI's in one year got my attention. The heart was turned into flesh to feel I felt my Auntie passing you brought me through it. I was made to go through my domestic violation looking at the pain and hurt I had caused. I don't want any one putting their hands on my daughter's after several arrests in different states. I finally learned that I am too handsome to ransom my life in jail with a bunch of grown men. I thank God for those ninety days the longest time back to back I ever served I pray I never spend another night in jail. I lost my job the day I went to jail God blessed me since then had and still got the skill to get any job I want.

I am blessed to be a full tie college student. I didn't need rehab because I drink for the fun of it. Thank God I didn't have any major ailments in my body. I thank God for watching over me while I rode that bike for twenty-one months up and down that highway to gain the strength to live peacefully. I thank God for it being as good as it is it could always be worse. Say like to my baby momma I finally told her about some of my past an I knew why I had never told her. She spread to spite me laugh with others at me but I even had good esteem in my addiction in certain aspects.

I trust and believe with all my heart that my higher power has my life in his hands totally. I got to keep my mind on him an give praise an honor to him for bringing Me through these treacherous trials an stresses, God kept me alive so I can tell my story. I have a testimony that only god can formulate an through me allow me to be used as a vessel To share my experience strength an hope. As of June the22nd 2008 at 2pm all of those past things just relived are all forgiven all are over and done with in my life I have to share my hope that a change for any anger everyone is possible if they want to change just start by accepting admitting decisions the next right thing. Jesus is the way the light and the only answer.

Chapter-3

THE BEST GIFT TO CHILDREN
FAILURE & REJECTION

Through my experience such as picking teams as a child, I came to believe that rejection was natural consequences of failure. That is why failure was such a scary thing for me. That's why I blamed other people for my mistakes, but fiercely defended myself when I got blamed. Some of us become perfectionists, some workaholics, some passive bystanders, and others just plain hopeless. The Gift Worth Giving here it is all in one big article of God doing for me what I couldn't do for myself. (It's a lie) Failure does not have to equal rejection! In fact, God commands us not to reject those who fail us but to "Bear with each other and forgive whatever grievances you may have against one another.

Forgive as My Higher Power forgave us all". (Colossians 3:13). The freedom to fail to make mistakes even when they cost us is a gift to give the people we love. This might be the best gift you or we could give our family and children everyday is Christmas. For when we give the freedom to fail, we also give the freedom to succeed.

FIVE WAYS PARENTS CAN GIVE THIS GIFT TO THEIR CHILDREN

1. Compassion I am not like those who have rejected you son or daughter. My love for you is unconditional, so I'm not going to blame you. I'm going to empathize with you my dear child. 2. Perspective This failure is not the end of the world. The sky is not falling. This is a minor set back, not a catastrophe. 3. AFFIRMATION (THE KEY) you are still worthy you are not stupid, or a loser. Yes, you made a mistake, yes what you did failed, but you are not a failure it was meant for you to fail we can't win them all. 4. Encouragement I have faith in you. I know you can do it if you try, and try again and again teach it until they learn it before they learn the exact opposite. 5. Forgiveness I refuse to reject you for your failure.

I choose as a parent to accept you fully, whole heartedly, and honestly, just as you are we are only human and we are bound to make mistakes. God doesn't hold grudges so how can I hold your mistakes over your head I'm not imperfect. Forgiveness is the most important part of this gift. When we as adults forgive ourselves, and confront the options that come along with that forgiveness then and only then can we forgive our children for not meeting our own expectations, who are we as parents to judge our children look at our life over the years if my God treated everyone like that there would be no one in the kingdom of heaven.

This approval opens the doors to a lot of helpful healing our children extremely need the most. Everybody benefits from forgiveness. Remember when you give up the right to ever throw the failure back at those you love. You can declare your intensions to your child to be whatever he or she chooses. Our children can then become a giver of freedom The Freedom to fail it is and will always be a part of life. Failure and rejection are prime examples of gifts of love! Every day that I am able to give God thanks for being alive is a blessing.

Each time I get the privilege to rest at the end of the day. God allowed me to end those relationships for that day. Now it is God's will t wake me up in the morning or not so if God's willing to see to it that I wake up again to regain those relationships I will be blessed again. I died out of sin and life daily through the image of God. Jesus who hires and fires me every single second of every hour that he blesses me to be alive. God's will for me is to live just as his son Jesus lived and died for my sins do that I wouldn't have to suffer the madness of this world. God's will no not my will every time I try to do anything I mess it up. All my teaching came from a natural point of view not God's power. Nevertheless all their teaching stopped working for me.

What I was use to stopped working all my friends ideas stopped working all my deceit lies worries and drama turned in to paranoia al my thoughts turned into schizophrenia all my drinks got bigger my defects grew terrible my pain hurt worse my resentments came alive my anger turned into rage my environment got hostile my awareness was blind my livelihood was living dead my relationships with family and friend women people in general was savage beast every time I looked up or down my narrow mind's eye it got bad God took me to the end of all my trauma made me lay it all on the line pulled me back out of the worldly sins of the devil cleaned me up through hell on earth. Just like he stopped Peter out there in the water fishing after Jesus died. Peter went back to what he knew how to do best of his ability. God said Peter why are you out here when you should be praying. God's son will give you a new boat a new sea to fish a new fishing pole a new way to fish but right now you need to be praying off the drama. Praying through this time of sorrow for Jesus died for all of us to have a second chance to get our minds and bodies tuned into his ways and words.

When I was a little boy, I was physically and emotionally abused by members of my family. I didn't talk about it to anyone, because I felt I was the blame. Now twenty-two years later, I understand that those traumatic events weren't my fault, yet the pain pursued me throughout my life. Deep down, I believed I didn't deserve anything else, especially the right to be happy. As a teenager, I sought escape in alcohol. As a young adult I sought escape in lust for women partying and violence. My guilt and grief would briefly subside but when the effect of the chemicals wore off heartache returned in the form of paranoid schizophrenia.

Finally August 20, 2007 I made up my mind that I was sick and tired of being sick and tired there is no waking up from death except through heaven itself. They say that you are facing three things while using alcohol and drugs. The three things are jails, institutions and a grave. I have been through all three just the third one I was a true nightmare of the living dead. God kept me alive so I could tell somebody in my drinking days. I thought people were showing me love the best drugs to sell the biggest drinks. I found out that love was insane and a wonder I didn't kill someone. I found a new fellowship in church and meetings.

This book Another Way shows that I believe in God to help me restore my sanity. Yes indeed I don't shout it loud but I'm praying daily for us changed people places and things going to church second row seat God keep me focused. I was blind now I see in the quiet moment of that 20th day of August 2007. I heard a voice say Little Willie I Love You. It's time to let it go then it hit one after another global pain and suffering people by the thousands daily taking and destroying lives throwing their lives away. Some going to jail some praying for it you can't wake up from death but through heaven itself. If I go to jail again I feel as if my children will have no help.

I looked around in jail thinking I been running wild long enough let me accept God in my life before it's too late. Time after time he's given me a chance soon or later he's going the stop. I can't have that. God whispered in my ear I love you just as much as I love my son Jesus. I heard him sense then all the time I knew it was time to let go and stop trying to help God do his works. I submitted my will to God's will. I let it go, before that day I had often sought release from the past but it never came. I finally realized that even though I had given my burdens to God I always took them back. I hadn't personalized the meaning of (Peter: 1-5). Cast the whole bundle of my cares worries anxieties paranoia schizophrenia molestation concerns once and for all on God for He care for me affectionately and cares about me watchfully and He himself will complete and make me what I ought to be strong and secure.

When I trusted God with all my heart and believed in His word like I use to believe in that bottle. God accomplished in my life what I never could in many years of trouble trying al Willie would have done was get drunk. God took in his hands poor broken little Willie afflicted from my childhood and transformed me into a mature and healthy young man. Simply put God took my sorrow and gave me joy He got the whole world in his hands plus little Willie I don't want to be left out. As I discovered in a very dramatic way, happiness and heartache are drawn from the same inner well, and the way we respond to life determines form which cup we choose to drink.

Consider the people who seemingly have a easy lot yet grumble about the smallest inconvenience. On the flip side consider the people who suffer a great deal yet are thankful for every single ray of golden sun. Know what make the difference. Life is never about circumstance it about choices when a traumatic event happens. It's not imperative that you agree with it, but it is important how you react to it. Even if you mourn the beauty that is lost you can still count the blessing that is left. This to me is going to any length to keep my sobriety just like I went to any length to get drunk. Even if you denounce what went wrong you can still appreciate what goes right. Since yesterday can't be changed and tomorrow isn't promised the reality of today must be faced.

And that is best done by not allowing the childhood to permeate my soul but by making a conscious decision to release my burden to God and accept the light He offers in its place. Heartache is everywhere don't ever think it isn't But God is always at work. Don't ever think he is not. If he is not busy gathering up those memories that are joyful and glad. He's out and about collecting those moments that are sorrowful and sad. Nothing falls short in the sight of God. Nothing and no one is overlooked. How can we meet someone we grow to like girlfriend-boyfriend-and praise them before we praise God. Who made man from dust breathed sir into a piece of dirt and made man beautiful.

Then he thought about man so much that he made Eve out of a rib of man. Whose thoughts are that precious ones no one but God. Powerful and God's issues isn't who we were and what transpired but who we are and what we are willing to let him transform. Indeed as I discover when I trust God enough to let him be God He works all things all things out for the greater good. Whatever the reason for all of us to be in our mess Perhaps tired of the struggles of life. Maybe grief of guilt has moved in and stayed too long. If so bow your head any time of the day listen for the voice of God. Jesus loves each and every one of us. Regardless of where you been or what you been through God promises you this there's more, so much more and it's all good.

Wow as I take a look back God has brought me a mighty long way. Honestly all of the steps scared me I mean fear of the unknown. If I was to know what was to be expected then I wouldn't put the real effort into myself you know it wouldn't be that gut instinct. You know I thought that I was a soothe jive street talking man when all that time I was acting out personalities other people around me acted out. Man, it was easy at first to act like someone then turn back into myself after a party or arguments. I'm 32 years old and in just this small time of reflecting how far God has bought me. I can say that 10 months and 3 days ago today. I was a self-centered, retarded, loud-mouth punk, yuck. Anyone who knew me back in my addiction can vouch for that and more depends on who you ask.

Now back to the lecture at hand this step 4 Oh-In my addiction I didn't never really want to pursue facing any life on life term things, such as my children I felt I started young so by the time I actually grew up my mom and pops would handle my dirty work. Sorry its the harsh reality Another way shot me through guess that in my addiction was life isn't fair. I put myself in a terrible lifestyle a very unmanageable lifestyle. The life style was full of lies from the delusional start and being so naïve. I was lacking in worldly wisdom or informed of misguided ideas and concepts that I thought up on my own. I jumped into a wicked circle of emptiness open armed all I can say for myself is things happen then all I said was the party don't stop.

Yeah until I end up in jail the coo-coo nest or dead. I'm living proof that you don't have to die to be dead, mentally, spiritually, or physically, and financially. During my drinking I found that I was living to drink and harm myself and others nothing good ever came out of the way alcohol made me react towards reality. I totally lost all sense of human nature plenty times I was in situations where only God himself could have brought me out of and yet and still I chose alcohol. The foolishness has to stop, no one can be me better than me, these are my steps no one else, teaching is repeating, drugs and alcohol rob you of your (RIGHT): R=Responsibility I=Integrity G=Goals H=Humility and last but not least T=Truth. Alcohol and drugs do not have surgeon general warning on them that's why for the sake of all others who are not hooked on any substance stay away from that shit you don't have to die trying if I catch you doing anything legal or illegal.

No serious man life is what you make it. Alcohol and drugs are for losers, people who abuse themselves to get a sensation are whack as the substance they use. If the doctor didn't send you home with it from the hospital. When you were born then you don't have to have nothing to make you sleep, or to be you. You are not who you are until you say I am who God has me to be. It's all a delusion in closing I would like to say my life as I once knew it is over God has adopted me into his Kingdom with open arms teaching me the pleasures of acceptance.

Chapter 4

Do I have any reservations about working this step? My reservation is where Jesus went after He told the disciples they wouldn't come where he was going. My reservations are Jesus resurrection and the crosses symbolic meaning in my new found life in my Higher Power I choose to call God. The reservations to me means Jesus has the ultimate authority=Jesus Humility in bearing his own cross for our salvation. The people spit on him, laughed at him, called him everything except the merciful he is, and Jesus still died for our sins because he is the One and Only. During my addiction I've had times where I've said that it was by the grace of god I'm still alive and never actually meant it. I was spiritually dead but God still gave me enough rope to hang myself out to dry.

Although the humility I faced in my addiction was nowhere near the humility Jesus faced, I can relate my situations in my pass to the reality of my problems and solutions. I was totally ready willing and able to turn everything over to God as I understand him. Nothing changed in my life I had to take baby steps even to get this far. As a child I was born and being reborn I must also stay humble as a child. I must sacrifice my time, my body, my soul, and my everlasting will-power to God. Give it all back to Jesus and trust him as the one the only who holds all power all power to be true. The corrupt thinking kept me away from reality that I had power. I thought that nothing was wrong with me, and no one could do anything about it. I found out the hard way that man's way got to many selfish falsehood, diseases, disorder, insufficient funds, lost appetites, emptiness, lunatics, and drama for me. What are some of the benefits that could come from making a searching and fearless moral inventory? You know something that's funny I always use to talk about a change.

A chance to change if I had If I had. I didn't know what I was talking about all I knew is that I'd made up my mind years ago to never live life like my parents. The benefit to choose what type of person I want to become today without outsiders telling me how they think I should be. The benefits of having broad choices are the promises that come from God for doing right. Why shouldn't I procrastinate about working this step? I just might find out that by working this step that I'm not that bad a person after all. I shouldn't procrastinate because I'm only holding out on myself, I didn't hold out on that bottle. I need these steps like the next right thing is to pray and ask forgiveness, strength, faith, stability, and the pursuit of happiness I love that line.

Oh yeah I shouldn't procrastinate on step four because my ass is on fire for God and if I don't complete step four. God will hurt me severely. What are the benefits of not procrastinating? I gain a sense of respect for myself and others. I will know how to be prompt, respectful, lose laziness, respect others time, and rededicating myself to a cause other than a pity party. Am I afraid of working this step? Actually at first I was terrified to work this step. Until I found out that it is my step I can be selfish now cause these steps help determine what guy underneath all the bullshit is left.

What is my fear? I had a big fear that I wouldn't have a relationship with my family and children.

My fears use to be tons of big pressured insecurity that turned into dust. After I gave my will up to God as I understood him. What does it mean to me to be searching and fearless? I must always maintain awareness of the next right thing to keep what I got so searching and fearless means seeking God grace, mercy, kindness, and placing all those principles into my life daily. Place all my troubles in Jesus hands and my fearlessness is no longer a vital issue. God has taken my fears and bought me peace. Am I working with my sponsor and talking to other addicts? Yes I am sharing my experience, strength, and hope with other addicts.

I call at least 5 other members of the group just for today I will have the uttermost serenity. What other action am I taking to reassure myself then I can handle whatever is revealed in this inventory? I have changed people places and things. I go to church and I heed the word like no other time I compare the sermon into my life after church and get answers to most of my problem. Am I disturbed by the word moral? No moral simply means conforming to a standard of right and wrong action. Moral is the next ethical thing to do, moral is the next good thing, it's so honorable that even the people called honorable believe in other things but this today means that a person is doing the right thing.

Why? The reason I am not disturbed by the word is because I guess I figured out long ago that you have to stand for something or die for nothing. Am I disturbed by thinking about society's expectations and afraid that I can't make it, I will not, and will never be able to conform to them? Societies prospective of good and bad fortune keep me alert to plenty facts that are plain to understand that being afraid of society will not be cured over night and that if any person or persons suffering from this disorder they need to seek as much help as physically possible, I think I've met a few people that can't function in society but they can cope in jail. What they can't conform to at home they can somehow manage to deal with life's terms much better behind bars.

What values and principles are important to me? The values that are important to me are as follows and don't ever forget them God's overwhelming peace and everlasting life in my life shining through my world like a light house, I value patience, the freedom of being able to place all my fears in the lap of Jesus, I don't no longer have to be conformed to the worldly image of thinking that I can wonder if it's right that I praise man, or each individual pastor for being involved in my life somehow some way, it's plenty preachers baptizing in the name of the trinity, yes they are all different people but there is only one Jehovah, Jesus, Messiah, Christ, Yes it's about Jesus Christ and being in obedience to His way dear God humble my way, Jesus said No One Takes His Life From Him He Give Life.

The principles that are important to me are the way of the cross All the ways I can relate the cross into my life for collectiveness, It's humility sometimes I overlook humility. The way Christ was being tried nailed to the cross, spit on mocked, made the laughing stock to the world, denied who he was after he performed miracles no other could've the authority of Jesus was so wrongfully overlooked. Now I value the principles of Jesus authority in my life You have heard it said before but I say it unto you He who hates his brother is in darkness, Jesus healed the lame, disabled, God sacrificed his only son so that we may have a second chance an it's a wonder that I'm aware of the opportunity to praise God every single time I think about the consequences of my behavior and doing the next right thing to survive this madness.

Now that I've come to understand contentment such as Paul, I've been blessed to have a few great jobs the funny thing is that to have any job high or low is a wonderful task, I've grown accustomed to wealth, I was raised in poverty, I've gained through self-seeking and lost, I've learned 1st hand that it's not about self; it's about carrying the message that Humility the way to the cross is through Humility no boasting no pride There is no other Name Greater Where By We must Be Saved But Jesus. I'm suffering from now on for the gospel sacrificing my mind, body, and soul to God, Giving back to Jesus and trusting Him as the One the Only Who holds all power to be true My Life as I once knew it is over. In Jesus Name I pray daily Amen.

Resentments let's see I had a lot of resentments before coming into another way for the second time. I resented my childhood life style very much I always felt that the way I was raised could have been better. I found out that I been more of a follower all my life doing things cause other people think that it's cool. I don't know I guess that's from having older brothers and sisters I saw what they did good, or bad and developed into a little monster all on my own way before the alcohol and drugs. I had 4 different grown-ups teaching me life in their own ways and now I think that that was pretty neat but back then I was one twisted little fella, cause I never really listened to shit neither of my step parents said and I've realized that my mom and dad could call me on my shit even then to tighten my shit up. Maybe that's why during my uphill battle to become an alcoholic they never saw it coming because I'd always bounce back. I had a drink and it's so powerful that even thinking about it back then 10 months and 5 days today.

I get weak minded cause It crippled me in every way. I wasn't this strong about myself back in elementary so dear God I thank you for restoring my mind and heart back to sanity even stronger than ever before I can feel it and it's so precious I'm so special and I don't need a drink to be me today it's hip to be square today, people talk about being grown having curfews. I'm going to keep it on me even though I want to shout at a couple grown little babies right now. We are the leaders in breaking rules number one the opposite of the addiction is following rules a small set of rules that you cherish would not be so hard cause remember only you can prevent forest fires.

So don't scream at no one when you get to that fork in the road and the thirst to use hits hard. Here we go Mr. and/Ms I don't need no rules rules are made to be broken yeah well isn't that how you got into the program. It's time for me to let go and let god do his job I'm tired of thinking out the situation. Now with God as I go through my day he has set out for me I followed his program. I resented my oldest sister for her act of molestation with me. Now that I understand that I was the victim and she was the violator my Higher Power I choose to call God is going to deal with her about that in due time. Back then we were just kids, and my sister had and has a problem only God can handle not me so I have to continue my faith and trust in Jesus and keep up with my step work to stay stronger so the pity won't creep up and have me out their acting a fool again.

Some reason or another I see people supposedly having fun doing they thing I made it look better sick but getting better. See Rick-James is dead okay, but the resentments and fears, behaviors, beliefs, and secrets are all connected to another person I use to be. I was raised up in a family during a time when all they did was have secrets. I'm living out one now that was at least 24 or 25 years young. My name is Willie yes but my grandpa Willie wasn't my dad's dad he was the man who raised my dad. My grandpa name is Alex he retired from Auto Specialists with my mom's Step-Dad. Alex has a big house in Michigan a block away from the college.

The yard is huge He's eight five years old a bachelor I see where I got my mac-cheese skills from His Birthday is June 23. How about that I don't know his last name and since I have been coming to another way I may be crazy but I don't know too many people last name anyhow. When I was young I thought that since mom and dad were faithfully in church that as long as they were praying for their household then I was free to roam the world. Well now it did not work that way. I use to run with a gang called the gangsta disciples it's funny cause in the projects gang violence was part of my everyday video, in the hood in my projects man my projects were sweet, Berrien Homes Property manager Ben Hurst back in oh-say 87 the projects was New Jack city no matter the weather outside if you didn't do drugs or sale drugs you did not go outside I realize that now my oldest brother use to be outside all the time.

I never saw any dope but my mom really got furious with him and I saw that fueled the development of a problem in their relationship. I know that she knew deep down my brother was trying her for a sucker. Now I was extra special like I said before and some of you may or may not be able to stomach it but God did not take me through it to be scared. I am not never scared that's how I feel now but my oldest brother Leon molested me to and then again I think I was experimenting because like I said after my sisters mistrust the mind-state. I had was very corrupt even then I had a thirst for sexual activity male and female am I gay hell no Thank God but for a while I ran with the flow curious George. Therefore I had the best of both worlds on my mom side I had a brother, sister who deprived me of wet dreams. Then on the flip side my dad lived in Indianapolis.

Man I could have had any girl at school yet and still the wickedness had a grip on me so strong I couldn't see past family. Family will be the first ones to mess your reality of the blind truth even then denial that that was the way. I have been saved by the grace of God on the 22nd of June 2008 at 2pm. I would like to say to the family living and dead rest in peace I'm so thankful in my day and time now to finally say. I have peace of mind unexplainable my fearless moral inventory reside in my God. No matter what has happened in my life they never were violent, I found out the hard way that all those young ladies didn't deserve my stupid senseless self-centered deceitful ass bothering them selling dreams I can't own up to just full of lies truthfully.

I actually had the nerves to expect females to treat me like I wanted them to when I wanted on the rag or not man. I use to be sick but getting better so immature use to low esteem so low that the feeling of a healthy relationship was curse words and loud arguments to the early hours after the bars. Man I remember I got a new car my baby moms who I resented most of all for 13 years didn't know who I was behind her she was creeping dude was in the car I knew him indeed snapped threw her pony-tale in the snow for what I'd just came from a creep mission. Just crazy-insane crazy isn't love isn't angry never love isn't your girl loving you locked up. I'm being as meticulous as I possibly can as God will allow me to be with him I can do anything my heart desires without him I will fail.

My conscience contact with my Higher Power gives me the courage to Nikao=Conquer all things in his name for me all I have to do is give it to him to handle. So for the past 10 months and 5 days I've been so sincere in my belief that Gods will shall be done in my life that I don't have time to second guess him any longer. I'm a true believer that there's no problem worse or less that he can't take care of I was powerless, unmanageable, selfish, hurt, lonely and tired. Now I'm relieved from the pain and suffering that I grew to know all so well. My 90 days in jail in a unknown city no family or friends just empty-minded alcoholics couldn't help me until I came to believe it was time to let go an let God handle my business.

My 90 days in Morganfield County restored my faith with my God as I understood him, then the next 90 days nothing and no one will ruin my relationship with God. I know of him because I was raised in church just calling on his name for myself, was a task I had to learn. Mom couldn't pray, dad couldn't pray, nothing could do it until I opened my heart mind and body towards God's way and will saying yes all day and everything just started unfolding one after another, powerful I always seen miracles in my life that let me know God was near cause no one could've done that but him. Such as God blessed us to make it to Indianapolis from Michigan while I was passing in an out drunk.

Living proof that people who put up with alcoholics are just as sick as the alcoholic my ex kept grabbing the wheel and yelling at me. My God I had my little cousins in the back seat, did I care no it was me my way my time. I could've killed us but God spared my life for a reason, I was shot at in 1995 a day before graduation by some vice lords, a gang in Michigan, we wore red and black. Our neighborhood was full of gangsters and we wore blue-black and ran the projects for 4 generations or better. Nevertheless I was mad these three brothers had it bad talking off the wall. I was at the wrong place at the wrong time just had a fight with my step dad and I always went over my friends house. My friends were Muslims, and they had different outlooks on life even though we were different in belief we were the same in the 'hood.

We were soldiers a band of brothers that loved you to death that enabled me back then in my younger days. I remember once my friend and I robbed this dude with a .38 automatic. The gun was friends mom's and all the guy had was seven dollars for us to split insane I almost shot o-boy but I tripped over his leg and I was face down dude was so scared he whispered please. I got up and ran to the spot thinking I had some money and it was nothing, well my friend lead that life and started changing into the blue beast. On July 5 in 1993 my friend attempted to rob this guy at a motel for money. One of my other friends had wax instead of drugs and the guy fought.

My friend had the slap-happy sawed-off 12 gauge meaning if you looked at the gun hard enough it was going off. Now with that said my friend told us after his arraignment that he never knew it was wax and that the dude chipped his tooth trying to rob him. The gun went off after the guy hit my friend he dropped the gun and ran through the graveyard home. Once he made it home he was covered in blood and guts and teeth and bleeding from the mouth my friends little brother woke up crying and walked down to my house numb. My friend that was involved in the robbery part was in the police car ducked down telling. He told what my friend had on His moms name the address the tattoo the blue print to the apartment house and the other places he might be at if not at home friend huh.

They went to court yes it was 3 people involved a girl plus two of my friends but my friend got 27 years to life. I could've been with him he asked me to come out there an celebrate they was drinking and drugging also we were teenagers God doing for me even then all I had to do was look at the signs. My friend is back in Michigan at a half way house for men trying to adapt back into society. We were all gathered together for his little brother wedding October 8, 2010. A moment we had all been anticipating for over sixteen years my friend had a weekend pass. Nevertheless I know he enjoyed every minute of the wedding and the activities that took place.

I resented my step dad so much I held a grudge with the man because my mom loved him I didn't have any control over their relationship and surely wasn't breaking them up. My mom is a widow to this day I regret the pass but refuse to shut the door on it my step dad loved me like a son guess he was making me stand up for myself by fighting me. We had rules until one day on my 16th or 17th birthday he came from behind to sneak attack and hit me in the temple-and top of the head with my oldest brothers wood shop baseball bat. I was so high off weed and liquor if it weren't for arguing with mom about why I came home like that I would've passed out.

I turned around into the hit in the temple then grabbed him and threw him down a flight of stairs. My step dads back was already messed up but mom told me he stayed on that floor hurt for about 3 hours maybe longer. My knots looked like cartoon bumps I wrapped steaks around my head and went to school the next day cause my knots went down. I never got my head checked I had major headaches for a long time after and you know all I did was party harder and harder. Today I don't have to be drunk to be me I can be me the person I was destined to be way before the addiction. Well I resented my parents for a long time silently as a result of the strict discipline not understanding at the time that they were doing the best they could do. Both of them raised 5 children of their own.

I understand that those whippings are the reason right now to this day I don't need to go to jail cause I did not like my family telling me what to do sure as heck don't like guards ordering me around in a 6 by 9. I resented my mom for putting my oldest sister out after I told her she molested me. I thought that was my fun time sick, after moms put her out she kind of shunned me to her way of handling it workaholic just made me worse, plus the counselor violated my rights and put the situation in the newspaper. I went on a war path experimenting trying to show everyone how to do what I was forced to endure, I was a victim now that I can breathe I know I was abused but I also know that all those females and family members that I encountered over time became victimized by the same evil that wrecked me.

Damaged goods no healing process no rebuilding stage just the world and everything in it attitude full of misguidance and no trust. Now I knew my baby mom before we got married and all the problems 7 years before the marriage and once she got pregnant I gave up all my beliefs for her and got hurt. I did it to myself plus ignored plenty of worthy candidates but I was to full of games. Head over hills for the foolishness I dragged my baby and my baby mom down a liquid diet that got old 8 months after the wedding. Retarded of me to go along with the marriage any way trying to keep that in-house and play around to until it bit me. I'm not scared any more hell yeah I was in love with her more than anything on earth and for that reason I almost lost my ever-loving mind. She tried to stab me in my sleep from having girls come pick me up at the house. I had friends, family, and strangers, even then telling her things, and telling me things. I was crazy holding on to drama use to it sike.

Now sixteen years later I got two daughters lovely, a baby mom with five children an out of love tried to have them put on my child support. Huh what is love if people don't do the dumbest things ever, in my addiction I'd be in jail but I got Gods will in my heart and he told me that if he accepted me into his Kingdom how can I deny those children they isn't my children but they are children of god regardless. I thought that I'd be going to hell for murder because my dad murdered a man. Thank God our judgment is our own judgment. I really don't resent too many facilities just opposed to the death penalty anywhere. Man no abortion either as far as all the other places well I've been to a few and they actually helped me so I can't knock the systems God created them for us to understand his structure if you follow his way.

What was my motivation, or what did I believe, that led me to act as I did in these situations. Well let's see here I was raged at my sister and instead of confronting her I started fronting with myself and pursuing mushu as if everybody with mushu hurt me. I ended up hurting more people and damaging more characteristics than I ever imagined I could never have been so selfish to think that those deceitful situations wouldn't come back to haunt me. I also joined a gang believing in the 6 point star that bought more grief than anything. The group I ran with could've had me killed a few times as I look back all the while all they would have said for my valiant services was please. I'm worth more than that to myself, my children, family those ones willing to help me in recovery.

How has my dishonesty contributed to my resentment telling other people lies expecting people to tell me the truth just doesn't work and I don't have any control over other people . Personally lies are all delusions and I loved to lie loved to sell dreams to myself and all others but now that I got My higher power driving my pilot light I can tell the truth for his name sake regardless if it hurts. Now I know that I have choices two of them and it s up to me how I deal with them. How has my inability or willingness to experience certain feelings led me to develop more resentments.

I became a very controlling person where you going who you been with what you doing now turn left who is that what you talking about why you do that stop go sit roll over no wonder they tried to hurt my ass I was crazy to think I was in control totally. Let someone try and pull that on me please there go the hulk angry outraged appalled. How has my behavior contributed to my resentments. Huh all that acting wild Mr. tough guy please I a momma's boy to the fullest, I am no shame in that but you couldn't tell me that in the projects man I was hardcore I was something but hardcore was not the word. I was a cocky now everything real huh a shame through toughness you can see softness quickly.

The portraits I tried to paint during my climb to be the worse alcoholic ever was watered down images of make believe idols no-one could ever compare to now I got my God to lead me through my dangerous paths and I'll be good. Looking at my part in the situations all I been doing sense the 22nd of June 2008 at 2pm My higher power turned all my fears around an laid them all out in front of me like dominos here my part was initiating the things with everyone else sexually after my sister. I was equally just as anxious for those encounters also most of the time just a baby once I got used to doing as a child that I was what did any one expect I wouldn't have a craving.

I know God has me in his hands I don't feel so cold hearted by discussing the truth Oh-Big momma's house there was this one girl I use to almost get to freak her she was ready to didn't take no time talking to her but momma use to always catch me pants down or something. Man I was at Least 5 in the back yard of the projects in the corn field on a hill tell you I was little me and my 1st love was laid out naked just talking not even touching we were too little man those were the days. The days of hot wheels in the dirt Kool-aid stains and runny nose, yep playing in my cousins hand-me-downs What recurring themes do I notice in my resentments Casino all good guys go bad, good-fellas all bad guys go to jail, scar-face the hero dies in the end of the movie, Never ending story the only thing never ending is the love of God.

Basically if it were left up to anyone else to help me up out of my sins I would've been dead long ago. My mom and dad put they hands to the sky and placed my actions in God's hands, I'm so grateful that my parent s went to church once I was born instead of a strip club, crack-house, killing spree, dope-man, I'm thankful they had the strength to pray and have god decide for them just as I have to now and its all good now a family that pray together stay together. How do I identify my individual feelings? Now all I do is reflect into my addiction if it pertain to the past and understand that I was a sucker for love and everything else.

Once I quit the alcohol I still didn't know how to stop that bad habit of lusting for sex man now I can stand on my own two and hell yeah it still hurt but I don't need no relationship to be the person god wants me to be today. As long as I got my higher power on my heart mind and soul my sight is clear and I will not fall short of the glory by falling for the wrong things in the unhealthy relationships that I grew so accustomed to dealing with over the years. I used to feel like I couldn't love myself because I didn't deserve to be happy. I was my worse accuser no chance I was no good I thought I was bad. The feelings I have the most problems allowing myself to feel are trust love companionship. Only because I'm used to the drama use to the wrong way things are not in life. I tried to shut off my feelings because I didn't have God in my life.

Plus poor lil me I never thought that I could ever be normal outside of the fact that I was messed up from drinking. I thought I was Mr. Comedian, a funny guy, the ladies man putting all my all in all in others before God. I was a stinking co-dependent, yep sucker for love selling girls dreams that I couldn't give myself because all people want is a little love to feel loved. Who or what triggered a feeling? My sister triggered a feeling I use to see people on Friday after dark do it curious so once I caught her in my step-dads hustler magazines want to see it lil Willie. Here I go the feeling wasn't supposed to feel betcha wow. I remember thinking while it was happening for the 1st time I didn't see why those women on the TV made all that noise, never knew that my wet dream was right there that I'd have a long history of tail to get that was actually meaningless cause just like the alcohol the first high the first time will never be reachable no one talked about the birds and bees round my house as you can see. My motivations were sexual healing at first so I believed.

When I was never as tough as I appeared to be I had a army of small crazy dudes around me at all times so who ever wanted war could get it still today but the next right thing is to stray away from that life live by it die by it just like my cousins 2-sweet and Nathan apple these two dudes and a foster brother Bruce man we all gang banged hard throwing up gang signs in the house of god foolish. Again God did for me what I couldn't do for myself each one on e their own terms met death on that one day sort of shortened their days living that wildlife. 2-sweet was the dude real smart quick to fight girl or guy big or small, Nathan total opposite pistol carrying concealed dude don't put your hands on him he meant it. Bruce fighter street fighter shoot later got to love him.

They were all descent young men just caught up in that life 2-sweet got to the point beef all over the city he beef with the police, sets, family, friends, firecracker short fused wow, I realize that now may he rest in peace 2-sweet died at age 25 in Grand Rapids MI he was wearing bullet proof vests plus the week before he got killed he killed just like in Boyz-N-The Hood Ice-Cube in the end crazy. Well Nathan was hooked into my Uncle Larry's cartel in nap and still would be if he were alive. Nathan's story similar but a twist they the other gang they beefed with chopped his left hand or fingers off and buried him under leaves in these old folks yard. Man the rival gang shot up the funeral show out and for some reason I missed his funeral. I think I was in the army and they don't consider cousins immediate family.

The pain and suffering we put my mother through I now see as my life without alcohol climbs to and all time abstinence. Just as it is said I had to learn that the people who put up with addicts or alcoholics are messed up true. Man my mom had to have god in her life back then that's the only thing that I can say helped her get through our foolishness. Knew that disobeying my parents would shorten my days I just never cared because it all about little old me, me my way my problems now. I was a raged rampage teenager with a big chip on my shoulder like I said I held all the pain inside that I was used to bearing no one knew but me. My mom couldn't ever bring me to ever tell her that I had sex with some of my cousins.

Man that I was used to laying up with my oldest sister until she put her out now I had to search for mushu the best way I could. Nevertheless how painful my mouth use to hurt because my Shaq-sized older brother used to be angry with mom. The only way to hurt her was to rape me or allow me to do things sexually to him. It's like momma said forget him so he thought so he literally took advantage of me. I wonder how he felt all the while running streets like hardcore but deep inside fudge packer in the house. Leon was crazy and had the nerves to take my kindness for weakness o-I use to do things to him while he slept hit him with skillets broom sticks rocks literally all I ever remember little as hell was trying my best to harm him with every inch of my man-hood I had in my head had to stop cause every time I saw women on HBO sucking dick.

I felt like acting a fool that dude had my mind messed up plus as a sexual partner my oldest brother was lame bum just lame because I had the best of both worlds I guess I can view it as I see fit. The next time I had a breakthrough I encountered my step dad trying to slept my oldest sister. He use to try to bribe me buy me buy my fellowship have me hang with him as a little boy I saw my step-dad kissing and messing with other ladies on my mom and at first I didn't say shit until I felt as if my mom deserved better who was I to decide. I learned 1st hand that people do what they want plus my mom thought his shit didn't stink. Wow another situation messing up my step-dads back even though I had a reason for fighting back one wrong don't make it right I should've been seeking the next right thing for my young ass way back then the next right thing would've kept this curious little boy out of all the problems.

Now that I got a conscience contact with God I will not be provoked anymore I realize the importance of the next right thing by all means. Back then in my childhood I use to find myself wondering all the time around family and friends, what did people expect from a little fella. Man I met people very nice people, everywhere I went school, the mall, the play grounds, at church, mostly females I took to preying on the flesh like vultures in the wild. Man I fell in love quick soon as I met females didn't matter cute face little conversation man I was in head over hills with you, all in a nice way with one thing on my mind even then hit it an quit it . But yet an still the mishaps from my childhood was growing in me still I didn't understand the red-flags until it was too late like fighting with my girl friend for 7 years before we tied the knot and broke up 8 months later. A record breaking wedding almost without president now I had 2 lovely daughters and a raging alcohol chip in me that until 10 months ago I never looked at during my service days as I was more abusive in the situation then coming off a dry drunk.

During basic training I explained to people that all I'd ever did all day every day was get drunk and talk to girls, girls, girls and party. When was I going to stop living like the best year I ever had so I thought and that year use to be 1992 I was 16 headed to 17 with a serious attitude, and alcohol problem, in high school weed head, angry at the world for no apparent reason all the time. Living in the projects understanding that I wasn't going to be in that lifestyle for ever cause I had the luxury to travel at a young age whether my vacation was fun of cheer or not. I came home and made my vacation seem like paradise compared to the summer life in the projects and even then thinking back it wasn't all that bad when I did what I was supposed to.

How often was that by that time I was already use to getting attention by messing up. Hard but true, in order for me to feel loved by my parents in a way that kept me from telling them that I'd had sex with their family members and all of it wasn't all that bad would have been crazy. Even now just picturing the conversation mom would faint, and my dad would listen but probably shut out a few things until he actually had all the facts. All I did to stop the violence and fighting was more violence I know slapping my baby mom was wrong but I use to let her hit me hell I use to be a big cry-baby I cried bout everything for years up until I was at least 8 or 9 seriously. The projects bought the Rick-James out of me I regret fighting her but I refused to accept a whipping from her, no way well I got a ultimate domestic violence on her when she stabbed me I went to jail 9 months probation and the shits still on my record in Michigan.

A very vivid mistake on my part from allowing love to not tell the truth even then cause she my children mom so that still doesn't justify how she tried to hurt my well-being I had to learn that over the years see and another thing all that time I ran with these so-called friends home-boys and we'd be out riding drinking kicking it. The police got behind wade, me Alex, and Curtis. Now mind you we all were cool but now wade grew up, Uptown in the city hood part of Benton Harbor city slicker and his home boys they all on another level. See and me country dude from the projects wade said huh who is Willie he got a click of about forty dudes at will ready for fun or war at any giving time. Man funny all this time all my friends hung with me until they absorbed what I had then they left with a pick me up.

Now the police got behind us and I was buzzing and everybody started throwing they drinks back on me pouring out and this and that. I got a ticket for it and all of them home boys said they'd help me out with that bill. Do you think I got any help hell no none of them. Oh not to mention the jail time nine times out of ten I'd be in jail only needing a little money then get it back code on the streets. Those rules never applied to my home-boys they'd say sit in there ride it out, crazy. I still got out running with the do-gooders thinking I was hot I wasn't nothing the whole time standing on the corner holding that corner up that's still there empty. Watching my children's lives just slip away and had the nerves to always have a chip on my shoulders about being called the dead beat dad my people use to call me.

Yes my baby mom she ghetto but regardless of what walk of life she chose to live I helped make them children so that corner could have waited. I didn't see passed the drinking I didn't know that then but now I understand with the grace of god and this lovely second chance at life I can conquer anything through Christ. I always knew no matter what when it came to the truth about my molestation. As a child I would close out my family or even the part I took in the situations that followed. I'm here to say it now that not all those times did any one force me into anything sometimes it was my edging the stuff on mainly with my sister. My brother Rico in nap that was more boyish like measuring out privates to see who was bigger you know, we two years apart so we use to be very competitive even in school until Rico quit an thought he was a baller a hustler a thug.

Man that did not work out for him that well needless to say I survived Benton Harbor MI, Rico lived there for a while during his teenage years and ran with his moms oldest son they stole broke in houses stole cars back and forth to chop shop $4500.00 at a time it was all good to them until the people Rico worked with beat him up for stealing they stuff an wearing it. Stupid arrogant he still that way kind of but that's him wouldn't have him no other way oh- yah my dad's other three children they were precious they didn't get the belt as much but still the abuse hurt them and they don't talk to my dad as of now. I always had fears that if people knew the real me then I would be powerless and I guess in accepting surrendering in my life.

On June 22nd 2008 at 2pm I do not have know shame. My shame is nowhere near his shame and grief at the end of his life on earth. Humility is exactly what got me on the next right path with my higher power with god I can and I will make without him there goes all that isolation and guilt and shame of what because I alive now to have a new day any time I feel necessary. The goodness and mercy of my Father who Art in Heaven spared my life so that I could help someone else with their dark days if I can do it I know other people can I got that faith in me. I got it from God and as long as I give him the praise and honor for all that he has done for me even in my pain and suffering all my days from now on will be of peace and joy not by my will. No my will is the bottle, but by Gods will his grace my soul says yes to your will and ways dear heavenly Father lead and guide me along my days.

As I learn more and more on how to be a better listener to the word of God, and accept the next right things in my life as the plan for the rest of my life it's not a chore it's a birth right it's a healthy relationship foundation of merciful loyalty no one on earth can provide. I had it hard maintaining friends because I was very controlling and couldn't get along with myself not knowing how to share emotions and feelings except for one night stands I was the king of broken hearts and lonely nights with that bottle hanky-panky. See I thought that as long as I didn't let the people in close I wouldn't get zapped fool I'm a co-dependent sucker that's all I am very hard headed I did it to myself but I'm trying to redevelop a sense of stability with myself to step out there on the limb but not like a fool like a young man with self-respect not to allow my emotions to be kick on for the sake of someone else.

Who is trying to get over on me sell me a dream ad think I'm supposed to just deal with it. Now I came to believe a lot of things and that's a no-no in my book now people don't act right I didn't I'm 32 years old and don't got a whole year sober or an emotional grip on the vulnerable character defects that had me knocking myself down to build up someone who was just as filth on the inside as I was or worse. I never committed to anything but that bottle and that way of life in the addiction. Now I see that and I was shallow full of self pity one main reason for the insecurity. My part in the cunning nun out of mushu was just as simple as staying drunk for free I'm a alcoholic by choice a washed up knucklehead by choice bad decision maker by choice all that and more were all the choices I was used to making were they wrong. Well yeah did I care ask me even now hell no and then was proud of it.

Now that I know the truth it's taking a little time for me to grasp the fact but I'm Not scared shitless any more not fearing nothing but the power of God as I understand him cause if I choose to get back in that life I know it will be twice as hard for me to get back cause I know now what I was blind to the fact on for so many years see God did for me similar to like my parents. They didn't tell me certain things as a child cause I would've handled them differently then. My mom finally told me that my dad beat her butt good then ran to nap that is why they didn't get married. See back then I would have went crazy as if I wasn't already crazy enough mom knew what she was doing on that one cause she knew I thought my dad shit didn't stink I realize now that that shit pissed her off and maybe just maybe I like seeing her pissed off that was cool to me back then huh. I can't tell her that because what she doesn't know will not hurt her.

Now the last relationship I was in it started off on the wrong track and that's just how it ended. I met her in Evansville it went from I got a girl until she got to much time wanted more road down on my spot. After that coming to Michigan but stopping before she got to me to see her ex, warning signs, all the time I was in Michigan player, she was in Evansville an Morganfield and I know how she is even with me that's her. Freak with that drank in her neck she turned into this hypocrite of my actions. Everything in our problems was around my drinking that had her comforting other dudes while I was at work helping her out. Yes it still hurts to recap because I was in live I thought I stepped up into a relationship that was based off how her aunt and uncle ran their lives. I am not no kid I don't need to struggle to help someone then when it's time for me to pay the annex for my shit I'm wrong all I do is think about myself.

Shirley would rather I be in jail then happy and free to make my own decisions. I can't have that If I it wasn't for another way and going to those meetings I would not understand that side of the reality of that shit it gripping and scary to think that there are people out there who feel that way about gods creations. Shit nothing changes if nothing changes even animals know when mistreatment is taking place. God told me I think you better let it go know mushu in the world that powerful plus he said you are a smart guy if you don't stop lusting with your eyes I will take them away from you. Put all that into your higher power and my higher power will fix it. You know what people quick to try man made things well I'm getting quick at doing things my higher power tell me to do.

Praying for my life to get better so whenever he decided it's time for me to have that meaningful relationship I know it's coming sure as he created Adam and Eve it will be the one. The one who compromises you know compound the promises of God willingness and the 12 traditions into the acceptance and our healthy beautiful relationship developing constantly not afraid of change cause the only person afraid of change is an addict or alcoholic whose in denial still that there life isn't unmanageable. Well I came to believe that my life as I once knew it was unmanageable an I thank god daily that he cleaned me up an wiped my tears away all I have is tears of joy cause he said I got you now. I am going to do my part and keep doing the next right thing for god will to work in my life.

One day at a time 24-7 365 man it feels so good to have peace absolute peace. Wow as I take a look back God has brought me a mighty long way. Honestly all of the aspects of living a new way of life scared me because I always got bored with new things. I was scared to totally commit to myself and desire to start showing love to the world that I had been trying to hurt for so long. I know one true thing it takes a tribe to raise one child. I thank God for allowing me to be that child who can wonder off and find his way home safe and sound again. My story is full of lonely nights in the cold, rain, and snow and don't feel sorry for me. My parents wanted the best for me the inner desire of my will power was rebellious. I would not listen to reason in my younger years that why I stayed under the strap. I would not listen in my grown years or I would not have the courage to tell my story.

If I was to know what was to be expected then I wouldn't put the real effort into myself you know it could not be that gut instinct. You know I thought that I was a soothe jive street talking ladies man when all that time I was acting out personalities other people around me acted out. Man it was easy at first to act like someone then turn back into Willie after a party or arguments. I'm 32 years old and in just this small time of reflecting how far God has bought me. I can say three years one month and twenty four days ago today. I was a self-centered, retarded, loud-mouth punk, yuck. Anyone who knew me back in my addiction can vouch for that and more depends on who you ask. Now back to the lecture at hand this step 4 Oh-In my addiction I didn't never really want to pursue facing any life on life term things, such as my children I felt I started young so by the time I actually grew up my mom and pops would handle my dirty work. Sorry it's the harsh reality Another Way shot me through guess that in my addiction was life isn't fair.

I was so naive-lacking in worldly wisdom or informed judgment I jumped into a wicked circle of emptiness open armed. All I can say for myself, is shit happens then all I said was the party don't stop. Yeah until I end up in jail the coo-coo nest or dead. I'm living proof that you don't have to die to be dead, mentally, spiritually, or physically. During my addiction I found that I was living to drink and harm myself and others nothing good ever came out of the way alcohol made me react towards reality. I totally lost all sense of human nature plenty times I was in situations where only God himself could have brought me out of and yet an still I chose alcohol. The foolishness has to stop, no one can be me better than me, these are my steps no one else, teaching is repeating, drugs and alcohol rob you of your (RIGHT): R=Responsibility I=Integrity G=Goals H=Humility and last but not least T=Truth. Alcohol and drugs do not have surgeon general warning on them that's why for the sake of all others who are not hooked on any substance stay away from that shit you don't have to die trying if I catch you doing anything legal or illegal. No serious man life is what you make it.

Alcohol and drugs are for losers, people who abuse themselves to get a sensation is whack as the substance they use. If the doctor didn't send you home with it from the hospital. When you were born then you don't have to have nothing to make you sleep, or to be you, you aren't you until I say you're you, it's all a delusion. In closing I would like to say my life as I once knew it is over my Higher Power has adopted me into his Kingdom with open arms. What does it mean to me to be searching and fearless? I must always maintain awareness of the next right thing to keep what I got so searching and fearless means seeking my Higher Powers grace, mercy, kindness, and placing all those principles into my life daily. Place all my troubles in Jesus hands and my fearlessness is no longer a vital issue. God has taken my fears and bought me peace.

A True story (Song)

Nineteen with wedding plans headed to the military/Trying to be all that I can/A new dad with a daughter/A alcoholic drug abusing man/ leaving the jungle for basic training/ You'd thought I'd been happy I needed training/An really back then those were my plans a disaster/I was used to running streets with addicts bums and G's/Shooting getting shot at in packs like wolverines/staying hype drinking day and night/backed up against the wall/ I promised my baby momma the world/I was wed to the lifestyle of partying like a rock star/lusting petty hustler for drinks and cheating/used to living a losers life dying to live/my stomach hunger was for the liquor and proud/a prowler for real the hunger was from within/ like the klumps at the buffet eat all you can/they never left without their money worth/excited to feed the appetite/I must confess and say/I've been tempted by a lot of mistresses and Mrs./I never gave it my best in any relationships/just the bottom of my businesses/ yes I had lust in my heart for the ladies/like Usher but I been a few more daddy maybe then I thought/I should have told the truth I just didn't want to/step off get lost this is too much disrespect/I can't have no affair on my lady/she's at home taking care of my baby/I can't have fun without her/I know I was out doing wrong all along/got offers to eat out leaving dinner at home/that was the old me I'm going home to my lady/God blessed me with a praying God fearing lady.

Chapter-5

RELATIONSHIPS

Numerous of times when I was little pleasantly learning to ride my bike. I was introduced to concrete for the first time in Grandmas driveway until my bike befriended me. I fell and instantly blood flowed from my knee my date left me in misery pain and grief of the scar is still there thirty-four years later when will it heal June 22, 2008 from birth until this very day I had not actually accepted God into my life totally no matter how many times my parents prayed for me. The only thing their prayers were doing for them was helping them to have a peace of mind. I'm in the cat-bird seat I know what to do now because I accepted God into my life and lately know it hasn't been easy and it doesn't supposed to be.

I made my bed hard now I'm lying in it. Boy I got to admit I not only see it I feel it. Thank God for Jesus God knows I needed him that very day if I didn't need know more I needed his mercy. I got to admit that when I was sinning there was nothing about God in my life no matter how many times I try and see it. Yes I do believe God was always close just waiting for me to totally accept him back then but the way my life was turning. I was a hard hearted foolish young man to a lot of weird things. I had no control over in the first place. Before I start I was considered one of the Black-Sheep of the family.

The drinking and resentment I caused on myself led me to believe that lie. I didn't care I didn't give a rats cheese about how they saw me hate it or love it.

I also hang with all the other Black-Sheep in my family that were used to being comfortable with doing what they wanted to do. I'm lived the life of a co-dependent so you can imagine how that went for me. I was a huge dummy you know what I mean murmuring and complaining. Who better to go around some more drunk high professional gripers. The art of family any way well that's all my family do the ones driving Cadillac's and Lexus. Still find something to be extra upset about. Huh the Black-Sheep list was whoever I was hanging around at the time. You were a pure alcoholic and disobeyed as much as I did in life.

The overwhelming energy that we had among family and no friends outside of the fact of those we all agreed on being in our social circle was cool. I fell in love with that from looking toward family after the street friends turned their backs on me several times. You know at the time family welcomed me with open arms even though we had our differences. What if they would have said get on away you put all them so called friends before family for so long. You know as far as being close with most of my cousins on my mother's side know mainly cause they are much older, then too because we are not around each other that often.

My problems been childhood friends from the projects, and Black-Sheep's of the family, off side from the fact that I never knew what a healthy relationship is I knew what one looked like, I knew who was in one but never me I didn't think I deserved to be in one of those. I figured no girl would be good enough for me to want to be in one. I was fooling myself blinding my own esteem then expected for people to treat me a certain way I wanted them to please it don't work that way. I'm a knucklehead to the fullest nothing has been that easy for me I have always did simple things just way to hard. Now that I'm focused man I'm know where near perfect but working on it some days are better than others. Now that I know what road lies behind me and that I got HP on my side all day. I can do anything.

My natural instinct in relationships with everyone else was wrong from the beginning. I had a warped young aggressive sense of ability to maintain progress in the healthy relationships. Most in part because I had grew up under people that never conducted healthy relationships to teach. I grew up in prolonged fighting, clashes between hostile and opposing elements that hurt my ideas of healthy relationships at a very young age. My personality was corrupt I couldn't recognize healthy at all. Growing up a Pringle we were special. The emotional and behavioral traits that characterize a person were never sought after I was tormented. The distinction of personal and social traits meaning a well known person I wasn't well known.

I was so afraid to be a well known person to my surroundings that I placed my emotions on the back burner. I erased my true beliefs and feelings of life on life terms to me my ambition and goals became null. I allowed my being to be stripped away by the corrupt unity of those females in unhealthy relationships. Example to this day from my last relationship I went to Morganfield County Jail for 90 days. All pertaining to assault 4th degree, and DUI second offense 18 month license suspension. Nevertheless, giving the girl the benefit of the doubt to confess the truth was a bad mistake. A year ago on August 20th 2007 I was arrested went to jail she was in the court room knowing she was still cheating with dude. Telling me I should plead guilty to my charges. My release paper work specifically states that I am not to have contact with the lady in question. I have 2 years of inactive probation to complete if I can't handle my problem. The obvious problem is that life isn't fare and people don't act right.

First off I never truly meant her know harm either way. I came down here out of spite I was just trying to get away from Benton Harbor, MI where I wasn't downing nothing with my freedom but drinking, selling drugs, partying, and hopping in and out of mushu. My childhood relationships also conflicted with those weird behaviors of me not telling the truth at first sight. Let's see I had two main girls I had crushes on back when I was little Janice Means, and Tammie Woods. We all lived out in the projects together. All I did was go back and forth from one to the next. Thought it was all good know body told me different see but watch this I learned this that I was very manish even then. My motives were bad for using those young girls was altogether wrong totally different from what they thought I wanted I was a stud.

I just wanted what I could get a shame now that I look at it yes then I was too young to know that that's what I was doing. Oh before I leave out another choice part of my life it's with one of my friends we supposed to be kool-aide stain share it all. Just when friendship has went too far I always knew that he wanted what I had and went through any length to get it. Mostly when it came to women I was the aggressive communicator man make everything happen. My friend was my bottom-feeder he always took to my sloppy seconds and I do mean sloppy man. Nevertheless he's a friend I will always remember as just that it is what it exactly is unhealthy.

When I was around the inn-crowd I portrayed as this stone-cold idiot. The mac-man ladies man all the ladies plus my homeboys played there parts in acknowledging that I was full of crap. When all those so-called friends needed Willie for the booze or the women laying wheeling and dealing with them ladies by the crowd load that was me some times I just liked to have company. Don't get me wrong I was a cool friend the guys they great in they own way but it was always a pleasure to me to top the day night or evening off with some sort of female energy. Whether I had a scheme for the draws or if I didn't scheme I was a born loser what can I say. I was terrible in every aspect of the life cycle and I'm sorry to as many ladies as I can possibly imagine.

I was a jerk a low life scum misfit show off loser. All these and more I couldn't keep up with the lie I was living that opposite of me thinking God would allow me to keep lying to me. I couldn't even lie to myself or know one else any more. Women came up to me during one of my life changing episodes and said what are you thinking about an I said know offense but I'd rather not extend our friendship level that far and she understood me totally. I felt great it was that easy you know just to be able to hold on to my dignity. God saw what I was doing to myself and those women and he used exactly what I loved more than him to cut me down to size. I can't say I damaged those relationships without knowingly doing it because I was trying to be slick all the time. I was sugar coating a cookie even smelled like a cookie.

Man, try to eat it yuck. I'm a alcoholic 24 hours a day I don't have room for being a player, in-crowd man, hustler, nothing else. I wanted from females what I wasn't willing to give in return I wanted them to romance me I thought it was their purpose that's what they were here for. Now that I got God in my life I see that my addiction had me thinking about sex never good thoughts a roughrider to it crazy. My desires were never shared from me to others in family friend or romantic relationships.

A close relationship between two people without sexual desire is what I think platonic means. Well sense 2001-2007 I have been up-rooting my entire life living situations and livelihood to be with so-called women of my dreams. Please in my dreams I'm right here sharing hope for the next generation that needs help in this area. If I could count the number of times I gave up the maybe next right or good girls. I would be happy living God knows where with God knows who. My life is going exactly how God intends for it to go I feel and believe that if I would have kept doing what I was doing then God would have left me to be miserable. Let's see no names huh cause I'd surely name them here goes in 1999 I got myself together somewhat to join up in the Guard then transferred to Indianapolis another huge move and decision. I took along the way a girl plus her 6 children I was madly in love.

Wow I left my whole family plus my friends behind. Yet and still no one really accepted this lady for me they had all sorts things to say what I should and shouldn't do. Then there was this girl lord knows I shouldn't have been with she had just got out of prison not for that reason just we had nothing in common but drinking just like the relationship before all we did was party and drink even when we were out of money. Needless to say I fell for them over the time we each spent together trying at the relationship. Those two were in Indianapolis the one I left MI for well long story short she dumped me not after I left her for a much younger lady.

Then I was working at the Gas Company in Indianapolis messed that up like a coward ran off to Evansville Indiana with this lady again you see the pattern as if the first trip wasn't lesson enough. Well story goes pretty much the same way she got to her home town where I didn't know any one and showed me exactly how unhealthy it was to be in a relationship with a fake person. On top of that I did it again but this time I had to go home and regroup from all the bumps and bruises of the love TKO's. I shook them haters off and chose another love of my life never thought about the other situations. Never looked at my real reason for this behavior even though I knew that I was meaning the total opposite of what her intentions were her intentions were to get me down here to Kentucky to show me a better life.

A new sense of stability another peaceful life with no drama now how does the drama king and queen not have drama that's all we know how to do best. Played myself short in the sight of God even God got tired of the foolishness I was putting myself through like man Willie when you gone start telling these women that you really need to get to know them or you will just shut down one side of yourself and never try an accept them as healthy when drama start I'm an idiot no wonder I'm on my second trip through another way see the first time I was new here in Morganfield that's it now I'm bran-new everything God has made new in me again I was brought a long way just for today I'm still inches away from that very spot but now that I got God on my side I don't have to fear it or act out about it cause I know that my fear is contained the power of the Holy Spirit.

I had a team of emergencies on deck for the taken. I had a huge intake for sex and females it didn't make any sense I could be waking up with one with one on my mind before the other one left the house. I was that beast that rampage over ladies I would get full of the booze then call them all over at one time the ones that stayed good the ones that left were crazy. I was ate up man just a man whores all the way jive dude an I up held that for the longest run Back when the in-crowd and I were in High School we played this game who could have sex with the most girls I snapped then in the 9th grade summer 10 grade fall crazy sex out of both pants legs hot and bothered. I know I was out of control you dig my momma even stopped answering the phone after a while she use to ask those girls what did they see in me but when that was only helping my game.

Moms stopped answering the phone she just waited until she met those few but many and said her peace then crazy again. You know now that I think of it as me being a groupie huh all of those girls knew what to look for from the beginning so I should have been like hate it or love it right. Wrong I still tried to at least show the ladies a good time regardless some kind of respect that seem to outlast all the hanky-panky. Even to this day a lot of females back home say thanks for talking to them back then most dudes in high school don't talk. If they do ask what about sex ouch my Daughter is about to be in High school this Fall Mercy, Mercy, have mercy on my soul Lord. I'm gone really need It cause my lust grew faster than my addiction.

God protects has creation so instead of me saying I was the victim the whole time yeah I was the victim of one act how many did I create huh. I was exploiting women using their tenderness abusing their beauty God didn't create women for me to lust over and prey on like wild beasts. God created women for man companion healthy relationship to live in peace no worry even for her nevertheless we get side tracked from the meaning of life all the time well this is my life changing year and I pray to God I don't ruin it ever again.

I use to hang around the family members that use to drink and party like I use to same old same thinking things were going to change. Nothing changed until I got myself away from the scene I couldn't see my way out in the mist of all that crap I wasn't strong enough. But now they ask me questions because they see a difference the difference they thought they'd never see in me. I probably shouted one time or another I'd die drunk no, no, no I have more bitterness and sorrow for my thoughts then every time I look back on things like that an pray an thank God for bringing me out of that mind state. My part in busting the situations up same thing I use to carry the weight of the world on my shoulders and when I get around all the more reason to drink them up drink them up. Insanity to the fullest that goes for all the people friends, family, any one I'm a co-dependent sure enough to the heart.

I didn't go around those family members if I had to then I would act like I was all good there was no talking to them about my problems because my best interest isn't in their eye sight. The friends well most of them were so messed up in the head that they couldn't tell me anything about what was going on in life period but drunk I could listen. Now they already know I'm not going for that foolishness. Mainly I just never talked it may sound funny I just never said anything about any of my life problems but what people already knew and sense my sister and I were already in the paper I told that story from the beginning to the end. Some girls should have heard it that knew me some may not needed to here it but now all women and gentlemen need to hear it loud and clear to be able to identify with the problem if an when they are faced with it down the road.

I have been committed to one thing for a long period of time in my life and that was drinking. I started jobs quit started projects quit lots of things I have never been committed to mainly myself I was never committed to myself never. Until this last three years one month and twenty four days. I am committing to a relationship with the new lifestyle of sobriety. I faked that faked at all of them other commitments to suffer. I was blinded by the alcohol allowing it to lead the blind side of my future for real. I was never committed that means trust truth and a whole lot of other things that I just wasn't facing up to. Reality hit and now I know that the truth will set me free.

Look all the time in my addiction I use to always start out relationships even with my baby momma with 3 main girls on my team dirty from the get-up. So with that said I did look forward to the mess but they never knew God knew that's why he sent things to cut my path off so I could pay attention and to heed to the light of things. Man I was corrupt for real when I was in the relationship with the lady with the 6 children she thought that I was incapable of managing on my own without her, the girl here said that crap the whole year last year if it wasn't for her I wouldn't be. Huh nothing for me to argue about she also said that the reason I left her house was for another lady please who want her hand-me down. I did the next best thing for me not the enemy. My ego will not step in like last year. well I used that leave hurt situation for her when I met her but it turned around an bit both of us she thought that I'd never leave her in the process of her hurting and ripping my soul well me allowing her to rip my soul in two.

I have been a co-dependent all of my life no problem. Now looking back on my behavior in the situations of relationships I use to give our goodies we had at home to the neighborhood once the goodies were gone so were they that's how I always been even in my addiction take all my booze over to the place where we hang at. You know no one put a gun up to my head and said go over there yet an still it was something I liked about being in the in-crowd. I place the feelings of others before me for so long everyone wants to know where they knew Willie come from.

I've had family members tell me lately that it's about time I'm standing up for my life well I say standing up in my life. I owe it all to God I choose to call God. I wouldn't e here if it were not for God it's only through him that I made it through my glory road. I placed females before my feelings so much that even they knew ones said that I couldn't make judgment calls for myself they had to do them for me. I feel like a big goober but I did it to myself as smart as I am only subjecting myself to the shell of being in the shadows of reality where people only treat you like you allow them so don't be mad when your feelings get hurt back for portraying like you know it all or is that person that cares all the time. I can't put no one and nothing before God. Who is leading me 24-7. I know that I must concentrate on God just as much as I concentrated on women and allowing them to get under my skin at times.

On the average I've been with more females then I actually stopped long enough to have a relationship with. I started out knowing most of them or at least getting a peak at the merchandise before disaster. Warning comes before destruction, I saw it first hand with my baby momma she was all over the projects knowing I wanted more than just that type I did it anyway. I was just trying to have my cake and eat it too. I got two wonderful children out of the whole situation bless they soul mercy. The one I was just in these last 2 or three years was corrupt just conflicts one after another. I saw the warning sign just ignored them totally now I'm learning from another bad choice I chose during my addiction that I have to leave right where it was a year ago on the ground in front of the house I was visiting paying rent and doing the up-right thing I thought.

God has better plans for me. I don't have to set myself up for failure any more it's right there in the dirt from where I came from. Keeping it real went way to far from a couple visits to Michigan to us living together. Until I came to Morganfield she and I had never crossed into that realm. The crap was whack from the beginning where you at where you going. I treated myself like a lab-rat stayed in the house didn't get to meet the neighbors nothing because I got a DUI soon as I set foot in Morganfield. We had been arguing that day cause she didn't like the person I let keep my 81 Chevy Impala. Chester Graves he's my good friend but also the stepdad to my ex-girl. So of course but if you sure your man is faithful which then I was so good. Why is it such a problem I set myself up for failure every time I went into the situations and God was never a part of the master plans. I can't have that know more no more foolishness. Thanks to God being ahead of my life.

I could find a drinking buddy from the top of Michigan to the bottom of Florida and back. Now with that said God has saved me as far as the earth is in size. My neighbors at the time reminded me of how I use to be back when I was in my prime dinking. Everybody lived at Grandma house, Daddy had son grown now daddy losing it drugs and drinking son selling dad drugs. Now me being a neighbor in that situation I knew all too well I thought I had answers for them but as long as I was still drinking. Plus fighting and arguing next door in her house hold I was wasting my time trying to tell people anything. Just blind leading blind they all meant well and wonder how I'm doing to this day. I don't got no answers for them just some experience strength and hope that they saw how bad off I was if change can happen for me it can happen in their life as well.

I use to work with my homeboy friend he was my supervisor and he didn't take know stuff off us either just like any other boss he did allow us more freedom. You know he wasn't constantly on you balls-to-the-wall crap oh. Well last year I worked at Rayloc and what do you know upon getting my 2nd DUI. I went that day to take the physical to be full time, I got tipsy and my girl at the time called the boys on me. Well upon that day she had me in the corner telling me that if I drank any more we were finish.

While she was out cheating not even out she was in front of my face with it and I was blinded off the chain. The cookie crumbles I guess now that situation was I was mad at Mr. Bill Duncan at Rayloc because I felt that I was a great worker until then I hadn't missed but one other day. Mr. Duncan thought otherwise I tried for work release soon as I got locked up nope. I got the shaft exactly what I needed I didn't need no free time to be out wondering. Boy I would have hurt something for real. Just thinking about it on this step is where it got to stay. See they made this program like this for a reason me.

Those guts back in the beginning of AA knew it would be a dude such as myself trying to keep all that extra crap from the addiction that never was mine in the first place. Back to the work yeah I was heated at Mr. Duncan but I had to calm down with the idol threats before someone took me serious and told the law then I'd be in even more trouble. I wanted to pull a Atlantis because that was my livelihood as far as taking care of me. Then God blessed me to work at Trelleborg now during my employment here it was kind of like a test to me to see if I'd sacrifice doing what an extra dollar had me doing or proceed to a job that I wanted to be doing. Plus my sobriety was being troubled very seriously every day. So I found relief in my Pastor Russell Wood who has been a major factor in my life in regards to my link with God.

So I went from making 10.00 an hour to less and happy rather than disrespecting someone at the job and getting fired for nothing. The next right thing for me regardless of how the situation looks to another person they are not in my shoes. See if I would have slapped some one at that job or even now huh. Willie you just can't stay out of trouble can you. I don't have time I can be doing a lot of other things with my freedom besides ruining it making stupid choices. I'm use to that crap the next right thing for me is what I'm trying to get use to.

Most of the people I went to school with now and back in the day are still up to the same old same. Prime example I went home the beginning of last month. My homeboys were at a open house for some High School Grads this year. I Graduated in 1995. I got mashed that night puked for 3 hours not good at all. Here I am 10 months 19 days sober looking at this in my head wow. My dogs are still living the lie just like I did exactly. That's why for that reason and that reason only cause I'm so close but yet so far from normal. I love my sobriety, but I fell head over heels for that life instantly no hesitation.

When I was starting out in pre-school up until 8th grade I was an still is super nerd-book smart Mr. book worm, know-it all Willie momma-loving Pringle. My parents weren't rich by far and my get-up showed. See that in-crowd seeing all the different fashions that passed by me so quick. When I started buying my own clothes with my own hard earned money I vowed never to go without the best so I thought. Man I still couldn't keep up with the fashion. Still now I'm so far behind I don't care so. Who myself compete for attention from the instructor the instructors wanted me out of their classes because I made them earn their checks.

I asked questions I did home work so much so those same class-mates that talked about my clothes were asking for answers on that test. I was smart I'd help out on everything but those test it helped out in the long run the people that wanted to fail did just that. You can't help them all some people just don't want any outside interferences. Well I was very disobedient even at school please believe it didn't stop from home to school. Just so you know I took myself out of Algebra-1 in the 9th grade. Mr. Webber K. was a prick I was to top that.

Mr. Webber I think knew I was brilliant but wanted me to dress like it. See I was all proper, super nerd sagging hat to the right talking all loud. See that's just it soon as I got in Mr. Webber class it was like I was drowning. Once I got in Mrs. Finch class that same week same class perfect. See that was a step up for me she was a lady I respect to this day. Mrs. Finch stayed on my case she even came to the projects looking for me one day. I'm like man she took her job to serious she pushed me and that's what I needed. I loved Mrs. Finch for that she's the reason I helped my baby mother get her Diploma. Ouch Mrs. Finch well my grades in math got me a job. Mrs. Finch applied for me a job at this Russian Machine Tool and Die place. The place was like 30 minutes from our city.

After school she used to take me to work. Yes she was on me she saw that glow in me that I lost soon after that I don't exactly know where I was when I completely snapped back then but I know I will remember sooner than later. Once I see it pure I will not ever be caught dead or alive in that state of mind ever again. I use to respect the authority of the people who showed me respect. Back in public school in my city you grew up knowing that little exchange could get you very far or very hurt. I wasn't the one to be just retarded about my respect level I did what people asked me. I had problems once I snapped it was on then for hours if I had the chance. I was high 80% of the time so when I wasn't sleep in class I was skipping school.

I was part of the honors society in school Elem-high school. The people in those were very enthusiastic in general they had their own sector. I didn't even feel in place there but my grades were impressive you know. I use to get a kick out of the recognition from all the spectators. As I entered the rooms of the so-called prestigious spots wearing hats to the right dressed in probably gang colors blue-black fresh to me. While the superintendent and other school official would gaze like this young man has to be lost huh can I see is how my first 10 minutes would go. They wanted to see my grades yup I'm the man for real it made me feel great huge larger than life cause that was something I worked for no one could take from me. Man getting good grades calmed my nerves. Good grades took me out of my drama while I was surrounded by so much hatred that it made sense to me.

I would need education in the long run I said it all the time during my loud mouth days. There isn't nothing like a smart dummy I'm in Another-Way, AA meetings, NA meetings, this atmosphere is great. I've grown into a well to do young man mainly because sense I become sober just for today know one on the streets want to hear my war cry. Behind the wall at Another-Way man and I missed here two in a row I had to regroup take care of some things. I got my life on track the best I can for today and I'm proud. I just think I have made amends with something I started long ago and just finally saw the light in the end.

I don't believe there are any words that peacefully or gracefully define Another Way in my book they are the steps to Heaven. Where would I be if it wasn't for the Blood of Jesus helping me to understand Another-Way is my life saving last piece to my cycle in life. The next right thing is capitol in my ever loving world to stay sober 24 hours a day one day at a time. Man I joined the army a whole year before I graduated that's how cocky I was about my national defense. Yeah right I was 19 young rude in every way and just didn't want to stay around Benton Harbor, MI or somebody was going to get hurt or hurt me.

Truthfully I made some pretty dumb mistakes in my lifetime huge ones but the Military was never one that I had a gripe about. I had expectations on being the best dad ever. I wanted my Dads pat on the back approval you know, My mom she's cool with whatever that's crazy. My part in all that is I cared enough to allow all that stuff to poison my brain for many years. So what how they feel about the things I do eat crow my life has to and will evolve just as God plans for it to unfold. I got the next right thing in God's hands so he knows my heart I don't have to parade around like a idiot. All I got to do is keep doing what works. Meeting makers make it.

Well now bear with me to understand that you have to see this from my perspective. I grew up in the projects around at least 14 knuckleheads including me. We did everything together accept bathroom 24-7. Now we got into trouble underage and millions of times my mom never knew a thing. We had neighborhood moms you know the mom of one of our homeboys that was ill. The one parent that would come and vouch for all of us wrong, even more wrong. I remember once we all robbed the Budweiser truck. Man that was wild the truck driver left the whole truck said forget this job and bounced. We got caught all too young to get in legal trouble. My friend's auntie came up to the jail to get us.

We were rapping and cracking jokes enjoying ourselves too much. Out of that group of friends let's see S-Love is out after serving 16 of 27 to life. Ready-Made is in prison 4-Life, Teddy-Bear Terrence he died in a police chase, and a host of other crazy things all from playing with fire. Well now the hospital stay in the psych-ward for me was long overdue at the time. Luckily I didn't Norman Bates anybody or vice versus. I lost my ever loving mind for about four too five months back in 97-98. I got papers and a story to prove it life isn't funny. My dad dropped me off at the hospital I was sick that sick to and didn't know what to do about it. My family didn't know what to do with my crazy behavior either talked about strong will power. I always wondered where was the faith, and prayer of my family at when I needed them the most.

I need medical help first before they prayed because I was on the verge of melt-down. When I went to the hospital for a week and got out I thought man coo-coo nest Jack Nicholson great. The craziest dude in the neighborhood now I have really done it. I felt a little disgraced by my actions why couldn't I have held on to what little sense I had. My personality was shot low self esteem with a vengeance. My interactions with the police were like after me and my step dad fought. I have to reflect back to when the police would escort me out of the house. Back then pulling me to the side and tell me to go some place safe until everything cool off. Only I used to go steal from the stores with children younger than I was at the time. The police came to my house in those situations the police wouldn't never go to any other parents door in the neighborhood. I guess he knew my parents really cared about my well being.

The Mayor Mickey Yarbourgh went to school with my mom he was the juvenile counselor at the time. Once he found out I was a Pringle. The man slammed the door said he knew my Grandma and Grandpa and that he was going to throw my butt in jail no matter what the judge and public defender said he was in control of my destiny. All along he had called my mother before I got there to play a prank. The prank worked well let's just say i stopped stealing from public places with young friends. But family they loved me so they were open season. I still had a bad attitude toward the police by now I was doing dumber crimes blaming the police for doing their job. When I wasn't running from the police thinking that was funny because I got away.

Man once I did get caught fro not running it was a huge reality check. The police get paid to shoot people who run from them if they want to. I use to ride in the passenger seat of my best friends ride. Yes Scrubber-drinking my butt off. We'd get pulled over I would be the only one going to jail. The police fault plus the fact that these friends so called. Just threw all there drinks on my side of the car. Man I was always up to no good in the picture got framed yelling at people. Last year I had fought with my girl friend ashamed I was drunk hanging on to the back of her Expedition as she drove down the street yelling like I was actually hurting her. I'm drunk she cheating the police get called they come two weeks later for that call.

God doing for me what I couldn't do for myself. While I was about to go to jail rolling on the ground in Morganfield, KY I was Drunk yelling at the police officers Yelling at her blaming the police an her they all were cheating together. I don't know my feelings were hurt. Now so nothing changes if nothing changes. The police got called to the scene they didn't know what took place in all the situations. If I wouldn't have been committing the crime I wouldn't have had to pay for my mistake. I decided to be with this female before I got to know her in this type of relationship. Now I've been in relationships before where the police had to be involved never knew why we didn't need them when we got together. She called the police once she'll call the police again and again doing it on purpose.

You know she said I (Willie) would never have left her if I didn't have another girl on the side. You know you never know how sick a person is until well I'll keep it on me I never knew how sick I was a co-dependent. All the females that ever meant me some harm they all felt like that about everyday life. I didn't do that misery that came from something or someone from their past. Maybe I just stirred up an emotion that made them see it. But I'm considered a cool fella. I just become sponge-bob to relationships. A sucker an I know it but I do know that there is also someone out there for everyone like for me right now my relationship is with my God.

Yes it did my oldest sister and brother misused my jewels I didn't have no privacy. So I held back from telling my mom everything like I use to an maybe that's why my mom shut herself off from me for a little while because she couldn't believe that I kept something that serious from her. Now that I can see it for what it's worth I didn't trust myself the most. All the little girls out in the projects had no idea that I was a predator.

A real young man hunter I showed bad signs of unhealthy relationships and bad intimacy every time I hopped back and forth with my childhood sweet hearts. I remember I got caught by one of my sweet hearts Grandma. We were in the bathroom of her apartment across from our apartment. I ran home pulling up my pants all outside they came right over to the house. Told my momma my mom was kind of happy considering that my oldest sister took something so she never punished me for those kinds of problems. She would just say what am I going to do with you boy. You just like your daddy that means I was crazy as heck.

Yes I said vowels and still held all the hurt inside if I was really sorry. Once we admitted that we were wrong and that we could get over the hurt once we told the truth to yourself see that's just it neither time did I lead with my God. Through God anything possible but without him in the mist of the problem I can't forgive the situation good enough to stay. I mostly tucked in my chin threw the towel in and all the sorry wouldn't do it's like moving mountains. I start feeling like I been brain washed and want to be just left alone. I know that I was as much the fault the blame seeker the problem stress yes that's me.

I know from the start that I should have backed up and said we should be friends, just friends. Know I just stayed going in the same circle trapped in the trance of foolishness. You know I knew that I was in a trap every time because I say I could have stayed with the other person I called myself leaving. I can do bad by myself honestly. I am just as the blame as the females the last relationship before this one I just got out of. Probably was my Karma coming back to haunt me down if not then I still have to pick a ticket. I done some damage to some females I know because they put up with me. Huh, I'm messed up but getting healthier and better day by day one day at a time.

Well know I didn't really talk around to many people any way. I use to hate when our business got out because I was so wrapped up in the hype of the relationship not thinking that she or they didn't see things like I did now that I know that little thing called anonymity. Oh that is so power full plus I was a knucklehead but I heard my mom say don't let the right hand know what the left hand is doing. Always works and listen you'll learn everything you need to know good or bad. While I had been drinking I was already Rick-James so the masks were all over the atmosphere.

You know what I fell in love with the fact that in those unhealthy relationships I didn't have to do the next right thing. I looked forward to the time period when we chose to be broke up or fuss and spend time apart. This all would justify the reason why I got all those numbers at the bar. The unhealthy relationship was my ego I didn't ever have to be in on time. Didn't have to be responsible, I could grind get drunk in front of other people children but then turn right around an get mad when my baby momma partied in front of mine.

I over compensated the whole fact that the females weren't on a level to make me want to change. Now that another way brought that emotional side up out of me and I can remember. I use to love I use to be so understanding I use to be so considerate when it came to ht e best judgment for the next right thing. Just because my mom didn't do exactly all the things she expected to in her life time. I was raised right an treating those girls like that wasn't good. I know that I was only allowing myself half the credit I had more potential I got more to offer I know it.

The major defect handy is I'm a co-dependent so with that being said I use to try so hard to be the mac-player, just in case I don't get a chance to ever tell the truth again I want everyone to here this 100% of the time I was up to know good in my frame of mind. When I started into relationships I wasn't know different from those other dudes hollering at the honeys. I use to run the streets and not every night was full of heated female attention. I really had a problem I remember that I always had a team of hitters like we addicts and alcoholics have different remedies to get high bottles or needles.

I had women just the same to me there was no such thing as being faithfully yuck. I was looking straight through them even when I was telling the truth I was lying. Even when I was telling a lie I was telling the truth. Man just shilling time away as did every guy and girl around me I was so full of it. I never wanted to be that way ever again never. I became miserable isolated compared to other men who probably wasn't proving half of themselves to the females as I was. I use to make the females in my situation think that I was helpless to the point that when they were ready to spit me up. They actually figured that I couldn't or wouldn't leave them because I would always come back and pay for the next mans mistakes. Truthfully I'm surfing all the extra tracks of the angles on this other side of this mess. I used to wear my dignity in my pants just as far as I was willing to allow females to get to me.

Then I started thinking that I could have a stable full of them until they started stampeding. I lost my grip because it was all a dream our appetites were never full mine or the ladies. We were all living the worldly lie. I knew I loved the act of being around lots of ladies and that wasn't going to ever be a first conversation I would have with some ones daughter. I wasn't that great at smooth talking any way. I did average huh where that get me how did that make me feel like scum a bum the same thing that I wanted to keep up under my arm. The same exact thing that made me cry hurt me shot stabbed locked me out of the house called the police in spite of the love that really never was see what our conversations should have been in the beginning. This me hey you know you cool don't get me wrong you know but I don't do much. I just chased liquor, and females not one without the other I got to have me some even three at a time.

Now this is the females that I became addicted to hey Willie I been hearing about you from the grapevine and you be kicking it a little too much for me but you cool. Well where you been in life I have yet to experience but you can take me there for the night. How far would those young people have went huh one thing for sure no children were involved and they already understood that this isn't the porch to stop on because it's shit everywhere on those porches. I'm so happy that I got God on my side

I must first put My Higher Power I choose to call Jesus in my life. Go with God not on my own cause I know what I am capable of an the end result isn't good. I can't send my life in prison because the females will rather see me in jail then free. I love my HP and He loves me I love my freedom I love my opportunity to find the true me through Jesus as I unfold into the man I was meant to be. I just want to tell all my new found friends that Gods love is all above all. My life as I once knew it is all over it's in God's hands. The only one who could have saved me from me was God. The situations that became clear this past year was meant for me. After June 22nd 2008 all that mess is history. Although it's gone take a while for me to laugh and flash-back on everything. God wants me to remember the past cause that's from where he brought me. If I was so perfect I wouldn't have learned anything from nothing leaves nothing. Now that that I got God ahead of everything I don't have to put myself in the mist of the crazy things.

Three years one month and twenty four days today. I got the best relationship with God than I could ever have. I had my spiritual awakening June 22nd 2008. I feel fantastic it's like I got so many different levels an even when no one is around an I start feeling down I get a burst of joy deep down that use to be empty. I know that God is working in my life I have been conquering many situations that just a year ago I was in turmoil. Wow I can look at the problem from every angle. I can reason with the problem then I can forgive my part in the ordeals. As far as saying I'm sorry I don't think so because my intentions were to do just what happened. I got in trouble an paid for the crime. I willfully admit that life for me three years and some time way before became uncontrollable, acceptance is the key. I have a real close relationship with God I love it every new beginning of it. I can keep my head up through all the pain no pain because God handles it all.

LOVING the New Life FOR Three Years

Three years one month and twenty four days ago. I was evil as the devilish terror that sweeps the nation with vengeance pain and suffering. I came to Morganfield, KY on Dec 16th 2006, hoping to be in love with a promising young lady, lover and friend starting over. I even had the nerve to think that the relationship would last for many years to come. Over time let's just say things happened things changed we grew apart. Her friends were her friends my drinking buddies were my drinking buddies. I don't know somewhere between player denial and isolation. I lost my grip on reality without know warning signs.

Just living in broken sorrow and a billion dollar a day drinking habit no one and nothing could satisfy. I came to realize this relationship was based on denial from the beginning. I knew deep down that she knew this love affair was damaged. My opinion was starting to become worthless my objectives and well being disregarded in the relationship. Love hurts to the very end dirty rotten and selfish if you let it. I allowed these things to happen being Mr. nice guy to someone whose definition of good time is closed in a bedroom passing the day away. I admit I was no saint I didn't know how to love until I got drunk. I did it to myself I tell myself every second of everyday.

Thinking reverse psychology will soothe my every vision of how betrayed I truly feel. All it does is hurt the harsh reality to my saga. No one is going to love you like you love yourself I had to learn how to love myself. Life isn't fare and people don't have to act right. She never intended to care for the best interest of the love. She never understood what true love was all we knew is what it wasn't true. Cherish me I said when I didn't know how to cherish anything but a bottle and empty emotion. The case of the mistaken identity, or the blind leading the blind, for instance I'm an alcoholic, living with a perfect person everything so perfect, wonderful absolutely no problem.

I fell head over heels for the lame game I was only used to that type of game. I grew to know all so well in my addiction to alcohol. Yes indeed I have to place the blame on something. I got fears of relationships now because of my own acts of love. During my rise to assume I had been in love with this young lady I found that she was bitter, scorned, and isolated in her own little world and wanted everything she possessed confined in her square to. Meaning she'd rather I be locked up in jail then free to choose who I accepted around here as friends, because come to find out she was everybody friend on the low what goes on in the dark. My love I hold so dearly is unique to the fact that I became the laughing stock of my own self gain, self pity, and I can't blame anyone for taking advantage of me during my addiction stupid is as stupid does.

I came to believe that God's grace alone wants me to be happy as can be whether I'm alone in jail or in a trusting relationship. I'm three years old I can finally salvage a walk to talk consciously with God. How amazingly enough God allowed us to be in harmony one day at a time we understand each other. I guess for the most part we came to believe that acceptance is the key to success in this deadly game of life love and the pursuit of happiness.

My manly image use to not want to hold hands in the park but now with God giving me strength and accepting a little change holding hands right now can be symbolic like a stone in the foundation of my joy and pain new found joy and pain. I'm in this same old world three years one month and twenty four days sober I'm a different person but everything remains the same. Now I can enjoy the same old park benches, the kids playing at the playgrounds you know tomorrow is the children's future.

I now want to be a part of every second cause every second gone I can't get back. I can see that tomorrow isn't here yet god willing I see it through his loving eyes as he embraces my faults and finds my needs. Thank God for another day people from different walks of life just seem to know me they call me by my name Lil Will awesome. I can laugh honestly now, I can relate to Dr. Martin Luther King free at last Thank God Almighty God is the only one that eases my pain shame guilt and remorse.

What can I say I know I can't close her out of my mind or memory she is part of my past. O-How they vividly hurt to see day after day it hurts deep inside see I have to ask God to clear my mind because the sinful ways keep saying just go back or she'll change but today I'm three sober and stronger mentally to realize. It only makes sense to see her face as a memory of what I used to be and what I use to like, I not like that at all anymore Lil Willie's stronger much wiser.

Willie can make choices based on the next right thing for me not for no one else. She's installed shame in my heart now but with the grace of God's mercy she'll be up in a cloud of smoke have you seen it. I'm going crazy O-How I need some more lessons on how to ignore these useless hopes of ever working it out with her. 3 years of self afflicted misery, nothing changes if nothing changes, it's a shame I'm a somewhat smart dude why do I feel like I can't cope. Sucker for love I want to be a better man even veteran's get wounded and need someone's strength and hope have you seen it. Can you feel it in my word's or my voice or even in my vision of faith.

I'm spooked about this thing called love can you see it why. When I know I can't do that because it happened for a reason. It only lasted for a season I'm tripping because I did the stand-up thing shit if it wasn't for this program and not wanting to half step with myself anymore. I had to stand-firm and let her go do her in that lifestyle I knew all too well I road that life long enough. I don't hold anything against her I am just an AA, Another way, Spiritual way, God fearing, Holy Ghost seeking, Peaceful relationship praying for young man now.

All the nonsense is for the birds I got to stand firm in faith in God. I know he'll provide all my needs yes have you seen it. I've been used to doing everybody wrong so wrong that as soon as I started trying to show how much love I had in me for someone else God bought me down to size. I can't be upset about my break-up people break-up to make up making up doing the next right thing God's will thinking clear making decisions based on facts and truth not false-hood.

Treacherous deeds thank you for listening to the two time loser because I use to be lost but for three years now I'm found everything I've lost God will restore twenty times over yes can you see it. You can see a new smile a new walk a new sense of pride and joy that just soars with excitement can you see it. I don't even remember the last time I had sex cause back then sex felt fixed. I could feel the presence of another man on her when she kissed me I wanted to cry, when she hugged me I'd stand stiff, I could feel the deceit in her body language she got cocky.

That's how I knew I was powerless over mushu and thankful prayer changes things. When I use to try to confide in her pity and resentment would build up in my heart like burning forests. Only god could set me free only god can release this devilish beast. The main resource that got me locked-up in this city in the 1st place. I was at the time of my life in that torn relationship where I was either going to let mushu be the death of me or take control of my life once and for all. I got peace in my life; I got choices, finally free from some burdens not all but by god's grace I will be alright.

I'm going to make amends and get closer to God and seek the Kingdom plus pray that extra prayer for my serenity in the new found treasure quest of love can't you see it. Yet and still I ask myself why did I leave Michigan I had to leave and go away to get sober and stay healthy. O-yeah I was used to drama for so long and abused alcohol my saga had me lost drunk. I'd put up with any nonsense drunk I never cared, now, now three years later sober. I ask myself can I be taught how to love. Please God show me the way to surrender my heart to the one of my dreams. I'm so lost teach me how I can get my emotions involved. Out of all the friends in my life today you top the cake you accept things on life terms you are sweet to the core.

I can see it in who you are especially after I'd just been played like a piano for three years starring in a orchestra I didn't even know I was performing in until she said she never cared about me and that paying her bills was all I was supposed to do since I live with her. The any man speech so I said any man can have this shit if it's messing with my sobriety and freedom. Any man want to dance with those terms may he have all the courage I'm tapped out can you see it teach me how to love show me the way to get my emotions involved.

The New Beginning

I am a child of God the person I used to be does not define the person I have become. The trauma I have endured as a child will never define my gratitude and determination for living. All I can do for the rest of my life with the problems I face is assimilate the mistakes and grow from them. I can make distinguished intelligent decisions about the situations. Redefining how I seek out all the answers by the grace and power of God. God's will is the means necessary for me God's way is the only way.

I can't live a life by manipulation and deceit. I had a terrible influence on so many people for that I apologize. I am seeking for more peace I can't give up and go back to that old way of living. I will do more harm to myself than good I assure you I was never good at following the in-crowd. God is more powerful than al powers on the earth I use to follow gangsters and friends. I was dressing to impress and doing all that I was big enough to do but God said not raised me up to do more than I thought or imagined. I became an independent grown man my own style good attitude and heart. I can't dwell on the past or regret where I came from.

The projects I will never forget so I can't be ashamed it's what made me to come to believe. I can achieve I don't have to live a scavengers life out on the block wasting time. I don't have to be defined by selling drugs or how many petty people I hang around. I don't have to live watching over my shoulders it is God's will be done not my will. I am a foot-soldier going from ashy-t-classy carrying the message f life to those who still suffer from addictions and abuse. I use to live a bad life use to be a bad image of self-respect toward humanity.

The total opposite of what God's intention for a man to be in his image on earth, I have the blessings and courage to speak my testimony. Hoping from the bottom of my heart someone hears my prayers for blessings plus God knows what I am and what I am not. I said goodbye to the bad guy three years ago. This is for everybody from Another Way to high and low society. Wherever this message reaches you in your time of need you are something powerful no matter what.

I am someone on another level of willingness, to surrender my will to God and to surrender my life giving God more time and praise. I got more faith because I remember when I was dirt poor still poor and worth more one love God's will always. On the twentieth of August 2007 I surrendered that day my roads before that day were all rough. I gained self respect and rigorous honesty had me thinking I probably shouldn't have all the things that I did I was messed up.

This is to those who still suffer and the saved and sober community you know who you are and whose you are. Remember where you came from down and out broke busted and disgusted. Remember when you use to be so high and ignorant you didn't have a care in the world. Who you were trying to be wasn't what God intended for you. Nevertheless the transformation of the mind and heart had to take shape in order for the process to take place.

This is who I am sober I have plenty choices good and bad I decide which ones to live by in life. I use to be an alcoholic in love with drinking I am striving day by day to make it. I try to amend my wrongs if I hurt someone the difference in my actions compared to my past. Another Way helped me discover who I really am I can't have it no other way. I want the sky from as far west to east in my saved sober living all of my life I have been limited. Limited to thinking that I could only reach for the sky I realize I reach for the presence of God. And he allows me to surf the endless avenues of the sky discovering a New Beginning.

I am saved thinking the skies are limitless and I can live comfortable under any changing sky encountered. I will never forget the precious twelve steps it took for me to find God. I can't disregard the fact that my God was at one time alcohol morning noon and night. Now it is God's will to take me from New Comer into a New Beginning with prayer and Thanksgiving in my heart. God made all my ways new on the inside things changed I don't have those burning desires. I went from being a six moth sober chair-member of AA meetings. To helping people break down old rules in life to create a new role.

The new character roles played are for the following new rules that work. The individual has to be sure he/she are ready to live life to the fullest. I no longer live thinking of myself as a gangster trying to be rough and rugged. I grew up watching people fight in the house like cowboys not cool not cool. I thought that was the African American way I know I am on a new beginning African American is a birth right for me. I was born again in the drive-way in the dirt in Morganfield, KY. Still so far from my birth place originally Benton Harbor, MI. I never saw Africa America but they say I am African American talking about modern day slavery and black on black crime in my family.

My parents beat me like a runaway slave who taught them that Africa. Those same Africans tried to trick me into believing they were God's. I am in the favor of God by his grace and mercy I was protected. Still there is pain so I am changing the rules. I am a African American created by God mastered by Jesus born because I am precious. God wanted me to look to him if I can believe in God the same way I use to believe in the booze, friends, drugs, and parents. I will be and stay healed striving to pull out that perfect reflection of Jesus being the best I can daily.

I have to do it by any means own all my dreams and work for my freedom. I mean it work for my freedom like I worked to get in trouble/shot at/and harmed others. I have to look deep in side the person I have never been even when I am down and out. God's will is for my mind and heart to be at peace he is number one I am the person I am. One thing for sure I let it be known what God's will is for you no-one other definition. Not mom, dad, sisters, brothers, pastors, uncles, friends, kids, job, nephews, nieces, co-workers, enemies, I feel good to be who I am it is truly awesome.

This is not a game I am no longer a shame it's a must that I be humble sensitive honest with the world. I am reliable inside my mind from the beginning to the end. If it had not been for God the Father of my Lord and Savior Jesus Christ there would be no me. My life would be weary and drifting like a ship without a sail. I am a extraordinary person Thank God for saving me and blessing me to be sober. I have rediscovered the best I am yet I owe it to myself to go for the gusto in my own self-esteem. God already know who I am and what I am going to become I hope and pray much success for all those who still suffer be patient and wait on the Lord.

I was blessed to have written this letter on December 16, 2008, The African American a New Beginning of Peace, Joy, and Longsuffering. I shut down for twenty two years of my life to stand up forever. I am a grateful saved recovering alcoholic the party lasted for twenty two years. The longest party ever for me it's over Rick-James is dead for sure. I was attracted to the wrong lifestyle by people I loved dearly. I thought as a young child these people would never steer me wrong. Boy was I ever naive to the worldly ways.

I wasn't even man enough to afford my own habit. I stole most of my booze form family members who were to drunk to catch me. Nevertheless I am so thankful God has forgiven me. Who I am today is the same person in appearance but with a new mind one sip away from being an alcoholic with three years one month and twenty four days sober. I will be holding on to my salvation and sobriety until God decides my time is up. I am alive for a reason the way I use to live was so difficult I can walk up and down the street hear the police smiling they are not coming for me I can't afford jail or crime.

Why am I where I am It took holding onto the back of a speeding Ford Expedition for dear life, two DUI's, fourth degree assault, and the threat of a year in jail for me to realize. I realized I had been giving up on God all my life. I felt like it was time to see what God has to offer before I cross a line I couldn't come back from I didn't want to die under God's eyes drunk. My life has purpose I am willing to try and find out exactly what it is God has for me to do. I love who I am today like said before they diagnosed my behavior as Paranoid Schizophrenic. I just got the answer I needed to explore it intelligently strengthening my ability to cope unafraid of the situations it brings.

They said they were showing me love by the biggest bottle, fat sack, please. I lived for death now I want to live. What have I stopped hoping for in this life all those worldly people, places and things that I use to cater to in my addiction? Please I have no hope in those things cold as cold can be not for me. The booze had pitiful answers written all over it no more hope in the binge living fronting for the in-crowd. I don't hope that the in-crowd will be waiting for me. They never were for me they were waiting for the booze. I stopped thrill seeking running to gun fights empty handed.

I have what it takes to keep going to attain my dreams. I do now thank you Jesus, I am a changed man reinvigorate, relocated, rejuvenated, and saved, rediscovering life. Very happy about whom I am and where I aim to be in life. I got my head on straight focused over three years now. This life is amazing I love it I love it everything and everyone around me. God doing for us what we could not do for ourselves I use to neglect them all the time but they accept me back in their lives I am so grateful to God for that opportunity most young man do not receive. Jasmine my younger daughter wants to work with animals she loves (Animal Planet). She is very out spoken wonder where she got that from huh.

Keiosha my oldest daughter wants to be a fashion designer, Pediatrician, cheerleader, dancer. I was blessed to inform her to go for it do what she likes because when she looks up from now on she has to be happy with her own choices I use to be a dead beat now they love me I love them dearly. Honorable Father my light my salvation whom shall I fear no one but God. For give me for I have sinned God the Father is the strength of my life. Who shall I be afraid this is to those who still suffering. There are those of us falling trying hard to make to get up watch this come to pass.

I am a saved gifted sober writer here is the prayer for strength. This is three years one month and fifteen days in the creation of God. No side deals with enemies I'm dealing with the Almighty Lord and Savior. A lot of people ask what's a prayer a prayer is what kept me humble. The prayers of the righteous are what kept me alive in my addiction. The prayers kept me focused on God and sobriety for three years. Prayers what saved me form my fear of drinking I could have been dead. I loved alcohol most when it tried to kill me.

I lived a deadbeat fantasy. Daily my children call me. Prayers what kept me alive in ninety five. When them bullets cut through the air I just fell and said a prayer. A prayers like medicine to the spirit it heal old and new wounds. It heals external and internally ask the people still suffering. I suffer daily I was spiritually dead in my community. I had a sick sense to misery I could see dead people. I use to be isolated in the in-crowd nothing but selfish pride. All you got to do to realize there is power in prayers. Just close your eyes put your hands together bow your heads ask God to keep you living right. Keep you out of jails, and institutions God please.

Please protect and bless the children save our suffering families. Dear God here I am I repent my sins forgive me forgive me. Forgive me for the mistakes I made toward others. The lonely nights I made mom cry the running wild in the streets of sin. The insanity of my humanity of my dear God forgive me here I am. I pray to God daily strengthen me I did harmful things in my past. I need God's power to wipe it away so that will never happen again. Prayers take the pain away I used to couldn't speak on it. Thank God I write a lot I used to couldn't sleep homie now I can shout about it.

I got strength in my weakness taking the pain with my losses. Carrying my cross daily I'm living on borrowed time forgive me God I am a sinner. Sinning got me where I am now I must suffer daily to make it. Striving like no other living life another Way blessed poor in spirit yelling save me. Saying prayers regardless if pain is there Thank God once again for showing me he cares. I will not shut down my ability again just face up to the problem sending prayers in the air. I use to get in trouble like a convict. Now I'm on my knees praying early morning's back to back daily moan and groans.

My prayers were going on and on my life is much better the best now. Peace joy and long suffering shall follow me. I'm on the glory road prayers still going on strong I'm riding on my bike or walking. Through the rain sleet or snow sitting back thinking over again. How my mom battled between me and my step dad addictions. It proved she was just as bad that's sad makes me want to break down. I couldn't keep a nine to five and wonder why I got three page resumes. I was living a lie paranoid in the projects of homicide schizophrenic ways on the streets of suicide.

I grew around booze violence blood shed running to the in-crowd morning to midnight. Hi I am a saved sober new creation of God it took three years for God to change. Nothing changed until God was ready to allow me to proceed he showed me Love through Another-Way. I accepted it from total strangers like the story of the Samaritan Amen.

God looked beyond all my faults and saw my needs. God has broken the generational curse starting with me. I have been relieved of all my suffering forms the molesting to the abuse. Now that I know I shut down from the trauma and unlocking my pain from alcohol the care of my being released is the answer. God has done for me what I would never have been able to do. When I got my mind back from the paranoia I was truly blessed as my life excels being sober. I feel three thousand pounds lighter it's a great feeling toe be born again.

I will not run from fear never again I will stand firm two feet knee deep in my infirmities my reproaches and necessities persecutions and distresses. Taking pleasure in them now because my faith based spiritual program allows God's will to be done for me. Meaning the natural man in me use to avoid them Now God allows me to share my experience strength and hope with my violators so that they may find another Way of life only by suggesting a new Way. An eight year old girl expressed it well.

When asked why Jesus was called the word, she said, "Because Jesus is all God wanted to say to us." I have taken pleasure in working on my own soul salvation. My program for helpful living has taken on an entirely new outlook for me. The preparation really comes from the grace of God. I started working on my sobriety three successful years ago. I had no idea what to expect I was terrified but willing. I know I was sick of being humiliated and rotten to the core. I resorted to the only thing that I could to help me get through this way of living writing. I thank God that during my abuse of alcohol I didn't lose the gift to write I never wrote this rigorous in my life.

I feel like I have been ripped open mind body and spirit. I have more mature structure in my life now than last year. I was terrified of my ability to stay sober. I had never had time between drinks to think because they kept coming twenty four seven. Now thank God I have three years one month and fifteen days sober. Which of my attitudes have I changed since I've been sober my ability to be very open minded regardless of what people say about me good or bad. One thing I've learned is that people talk about people good or bad.

So I use to think in my closed circle no one could feel my pain the tug of war of living in denial needed to be broken up. I was al ready use to living spiritually dead to death. I could get right in the sight of God. Plenty times over I could have killed or been killed driving drunk. All those people that have lost their lives and family because of alcohol related issues could have been me. Thank God I am still here to tell someone about my poor judgments and experiences. I just maybe able to help someone by expressing my strength and hope for people suffering from lack of ambition.

The tragic things that happened in my life are the best things that ever happened in my life. I wouldn't go back and change a thing. Those situations made me who I am today God bought me up out all that darkness to be able to share the pain. Tell some other people who maybe having ordeals they dealing with that its going to be alright. Just take if one day at a time I was diagnosed with being a Paranoid Schizophrenic back in ninety eight. I had been called worse than that in my day and time. I told the doctor they were the one crazy. I took a trip to the psych-ward for a little while to cool down.

I got some rest for about a week went straight to the liquor store. After that ordeal my drinking went to the ceiling I blamed it on the weed to drink more. I can do al things through Christ who strengthens me. I have been blessed to be able to get help in working on my problems to keep them at a minimal. I realize that staying focused on my sobriety calls for me to go beyond the call of duty. I must delve into the pains source making for a better person I aim to become. I am not scared of tackling situations that use to hurt me as long as I am sober. I am very teachable in all avenues I learn on my own from others old or young.

It's such a wonderful thing to not be in control and know that God has the power in his hands. Just to be able to follow that is amazing for me because I can remember like yesterday I was ate up to the core. Now I have a peace of mind I don't want to lose for a hundred million dollars. Nothing compares to God's will for my life no one nothing not nothing. Where has the over-blown been deflated-The pity party are gone with the wind please I am sober sure I can look back and say me, me, me.

The point is I deserve what I got out of all that non-sense the pay back comes with the turf. Just some people enjoy keeping there story to themselves. Well I was talking drunk so guess what I am a grateful saved sober man. I do not know it all I don't know to little. I know exactly what God wants me to know to keep moving forward day by day. I don't praise the wrong things in life and more. I am a stronger co-dependent these days all the credit goes to God. The people that use to get credit from me please they are who they are no more or less.

My salvation and sobriety is mine all by myself I can be stingy with it whenever I choose to be gaining strength for me only sharing experience and hope. I am much more encouraging to people now than ever because other people need to really give their all to God and sobriety to heal. I never loved myself as much as I do now I never thought I was supposed to love myself because no one ever practiced loving themselves around me. Still to this day people I use to look up to don't love them enough to give God the glory and Honor. I am deflated in being the drama king no more hassle no more wanting to be miserable. No more barking out loud obscene rudeness in public acting a fool.

I take pride in handling myself as a mature young adult. I surrendered to it day to day God please bless my enemies mainly me. Where ahs the healthy part of me been uncovered. Through my trauma the same things that got me here are shutting down emotionally from pain. I have opened up and got out of my own way placed all my problems in god's hands daily it is not easy. I got to stay focused and gain all the knowledge about God. The next level for me will be manageable for my life. I can still find ways to have peace it hurts but it isn't near hurtful as my drinking days. The healthy discovery of my life is that I am more affectionate toward life.

I watch views of nature more now then ever the sunset, sun rise. I see views of big cities the landscapes and designs as art. I see dew drops on blades of grass and leaves that amazes me. I love being sober and in my children life I am not rich but I don't have to be rich to rule this world. I know that's prince but it is true that's how I feel right now. I love the person sobriety shaped me to be nothing can come between my sobriety is how I feel. Blood is thicker than water yeah if I get a cup of water and drink it. The water is in my body thinning my blood my blood doesn't pump for no one else.

My blood pumps for the love of God the Father of my lord and savior Jesus Christ. If someone were to hit me in the jaw today I would give him the other one. I can honestly say that today three years ago I couldn't say that. How does humility affect my sobriety? I use to say I got the patience of job that is a no-no. I can more relate to the story of Joseph in (God with Us). Emmanuel means God with us I was living dead for so long God opened up his kingdom to me.

I was in Henderson, KY June twenty second 2008 at the Mandarin Chinese at two pm. I started crying tears of joy it was awesome I have been growing stronger in God's will being truly blessed. I have incorporated the love of God into my lifestyle it is a new richness. You know the bitter sweetness in my alcoholism I was as proud as a peacock. I took pride in pleasing others not God I took pride in the in-crowd. I did humiliating things to myself to impress other people who accepted me for nothing less then to make a complete fool out of myself. I could careless what they think I been to the psych-ward and back.

I been to jails plenty times and back them same friends are still there doing the same old stuff. I was trying to justify my drinking those were man's laws and rules. God's grace and mercy calls for forgiveness justice and mercy meets for all of us at the cross if I believe. God has control and his way is sufficient always. Humility affects my recovery because I have returned form refuge out of my distress and I feel like an eagle above the clouds of eh storm. Remarkable when I was a child then God loved me and gave me more strength then at age twenty two.

Now twenty two years later I think to all circumstances of those involved in my trauma. Regardless of the pain we are all family and that is just that we got to work out things good or bad. We must find out how to get along through all things good or bad being humble is a command form God I am no longer to take it for granted. I am to esteem others better than myself humble myself god resist the proud, grace comes to the humble. Not preaching but Jesus became a man he humbled himself Philippians 2:5-8) I have to be setting an example for others to follow.

I can finally see real reachable values through reality. First I had to regain my confidence back I don't know where it slipped off to I didn't even see it leave. I got t back now I must stay focused on God I can't admire people places or things for wealth. I got to learn through my humility with things have true eternal value. Humility first of all doesn't mean upset just like blessed don't mean pity or sympathy. Blessed and humility are congratulations' job well done. People with humility in God's eyes are better off in eh long run.

I am aware of my own guilt sins bankruptcy problems divorce needs. I got to turn to God for help self righteous are destroyed. The lowly and saved I will be not proud being meek and humble is having strength reined inside. The meek Jesus is certainly no weakling. Humility in my life allows God to take my steering wheel. How has my understanding of God grown in the previous years? I am here by the grace of God it was preordained by God. I am firm in my beliefs my faith fight is awesome. I've had the privileged of bringing the message to my dad he raised me in church only to try and give up on God didn't leave us hanging.

The Morphine almost killed my dad recently I expressed my deep concern to my dad. Through the story of King Hezekiah he took ill and was on his death bed jut like my dad. The doctor Isaiah saw Hezekiah as I did my dad lifeless trying to give up. Thank God for my sobriety I was able to speak intelligently enough to my dad. I extended my hand to him so that he can regain strength. My dad was also tripping trying to play God which was no surprise to me. I remember a few of my episodes the devil is a liar god has me exactly where I am in my life for a reason.

Until Hezekiah turned his face to the wall and cried out to god he couldn't get healed. I told my dad that there is no waking up from death except through heaven. He looked at my every move it was hard seeing him that way but it had to happen. I also told him that tough guy image doesn't impress anyone anymore that was back in his prime leave it back there. God sees us form beginning to end all in one glance no hiding. No one else in the world can do that so therefore get out of your own way and let God do for you what you certainly can't do for yourself.

I have been firm in my status having faith patiently waiting for deliverance out of my slump I put myself in see. Everything was freely given to me years ago this time I got to put in some work because God got me on his team. I am fairly new to learning and understanding because I played God for a while it didn't work. Myself will ran out I snapped I learned that's why God is awesome. Making sure people act right is a hard job especially when I use to be a knucklehead and still just remembering my days woo.

Thinking about those out there god's watching over some make it some don't ouch. It's true enough to allow me to stay true to me. I must stay as active in sobriety as I did in my drinking days. I now know that everyday is another precious moment I get to give my life over to the care of God as I understand him. I wake up daily meditating and praying and reading my bible soon as I get up. I also ask that he lead and guide me don't allow any hurt harm or danger to come upon me. Do not allow me to hurt anyone regardless of where I may be. I don't have to shut down any longer every time I say it or here shut down I get a boost of energy. I have so much gratitude for the entire program from Another Way.

I was able to build a foundation to stand on in my life finally that rebuilds my ability to live as I should right and not how someone else perceives for me to live. I am a strong peace seeker from now on seeking for peace in everything that I do. How will I ask God to remove my shortcomings? I will get down on my rusty knees every morn, noon, and night and ask God to help me. I can't make it on my own I need him in my life. Our Father forgives our foolish pride. Remind me of your providential care so that I will not trust in myself in the name of my Lord and Savior Jesus Christ. Amen.

Our Father I admit my weakness and sinfulness. Help me to change my heart and mend my ways. May we always be a community of repentance eager to hear your voice and to follow your will? In Christ's Name I pray amen. The gift of sobriety is other people sharing their life experiences to help others. God works in mysterious ways through fellowship of people and God's will each of us have as we get in tune with that part and spread the message to others who still suffer. I got adopted into this new way of life and got a healthy network of family in sobriety.

I started out new sharing whether people wanted to hear it or not. I got the relief I was praying for and every time I go to church or meeting I will always hear or say something that is needed. I have a wonderful pastor as a mentor preaching the word no sugar coating. I have to learn how to get out of the way of myself. How does the spiritual principal of surrender apply to getting out of the way so God can work in our lives?

Every resource I ever had in the world stopped working for me and my mind didn't want anything else. I didn't have mom as a crutch for a healthy dude enabled me to death. No money couldn't help me no one I almost got a year in the county jail three hundred days. Who me oh lord please not me don't let this happen I am not the smartest. I don't need a year to think about it either I quit drinking it's over we are divorced. Now anything that wants to come in between that divorce got to go relationship also because unhealthy relationships are not worth me going back to jail or holding onto speeding trucks.

Super-stupid sucker for love knucklehead to the bone there is something about the dirt in Morganfield, KY that changed my life on August 20, 2007. Plus the ex-girlfriend yelling it's over I hate you piece of crap you think I wasn't upset at myself and her. Well we tried falling does hurt getting up hurts but God's will be done it is even easier. I can brush the dirt off my shoulders and breathe. I was powerless over everything my actions were played like a fiddle because I wore it on my sleeve. Now I got God's protection and he only wants the best for me. So I am ready I surrender Lord I am not a criminal I was playing tough.

Lord alcohol doesn't even taste good I was just copying off people I saw do it and liked it. Please forgive me for all my wicked ways lord I will place my all in your hands. I have tried everything once all types of booze, girls, games. Dear God please help nothing work everything else stopped. Thy will be done is everlasting to everlasting. How has my surrender deepened? I wake up thanking God because I got a right to it's in my soul. I just feel complete all day he's on my mind, when I go to sleep. I am thankful in all my ways that God had allowed me too live. I can't express it more it is awesome to be able to pray for about an hour. Good things come to those who wait on the lord with all earnestness of heart.

What might be the benefit of allowing God to work in my life? I will be meek well gentle that's a good benefit. Those who mourn shall receive God's favor those who mourn for their own spiritual sinfulness will be comforted by the grace and forgiveness of God. You know I came from the inner city so that's who I am addressing. They may sneer at the promise the meek shall inherit the earth. But as heirs of God and joint heirs with Christ, the children of God will ultimately inherit all things. I have a burning zeal and unsatisfied appetite to pursue what is right.

The world left me disappointed and unsatisfied; I was tired of living in insanity. By asking God to take over my hunger and thirst will be filled by coming to God my slate was wiped clean. How do I feel knowing that God is caring for me and working in my life? I feel merciful forgiving to people who have wronged me. I guess you'd say I have a generous spirit. Either way if I am a sinner/or afflicted person I will be shown mercy.

You know people who are not merciful or forgiving to others can't expect God to be merciful and forgiving to them I feel a great peaceful shield over me. I am trying to live at peace with all breaking down the walls of hostility and to be a servant of reconcile. I am a child of God cause now I value peace. Seek it pursue it. Spiritual Principles I do not have control over anything but my own actions and thinking. I was still walking and riding my bike any place I needed to go. I learned that it was my fault that I had two DUI's. I can't help that other people hurt me I was hurting them as well.

I am allergic to alcohol so therefore I can't be around people in my past who think it's cool. I am still in a financial bind but in my drinking days I would be trying to do something to get money the wrong way. SO I need to design me a plan to get the proper job that will go with my hours I need around school. I never wanted to alone naturally who does. I just didn't know what I wanted I didn't love myself. I couldn't love anyone else miserable for no reason. Now that I came to a decision in my life to take a stand it takes some getting use to. I will be alright I got self respect it left when I was eighteen years old. I am not in a hurry any more patience is a virtue.

I am feeling better already I got a psychiatrist, pastors, minister, church mother's and deacons to aid in my foundation of the shut down. So that I can get to the core of that problem I am steady on the case of my eternal destiny. Very open minded willing and able to be a success in every aspect of my life. I know God strengthens them as a result of working out my soul salvation. I know God strengthens me daily and I gain answers to strong holds in my ability that once I get them I am set free to build another avenue up another stair toward my ultimate peak. I am peaking I am not at my climax in life you know I am still playing Basketball, Flipping, and riding a bike.

Only God can remove my shortcomings first you got to do things to accept him into your matter peacefully ask not in a battle understand how he works before you try to work him. The first few months of my sobriety I still tried to play God it didn't work. Until I humbly asked God to help me surrender all I had to do was keep thinking back to instances where I was certainly not in control of anything in my life. When I surrendered I still found out that I didn't have any control over nothing but me. If something about someone else was bothering me there is something wrong with me. I am living on borrowed time God's will for me is to wait patiently on him comes along the lines of long suffering joy comes early.

I might not have I now but I'm prayed up I might not be banking but God knows what I need when I need it. God will make a way some how it's not up to me to question I can pursue the next right thing and do right putting forth the effort God will give me the boost I need. Actually my sense of proportion use to be out of whack. I had to shed things cut off things in order to stop getting outside the box. My perspective is all reachable added with a little responsibility on my part to be the best.

I can so I must stop holding back on my desires for me and stay focused on the right thing. Plus stay on the task at hand stay prayed up and above water with peace. I went to visit a friend in jail and he's so full of himself like I use to be at that age. I had to tell him that tough guy non-sense doesn't impress me for some reason that works. Nevertheless I avoid those visits unless I have to relay a message form now on because that is his fault and I met him in jail in 2007. So he's back in jail knucklehead I will not allow that to pull me off my square. I have been doing well I haven't been getting called out my name every things going wrong it's my entire fault.

I am so much more calm and patient God doing for me loving it. I no longer mascot for the in-crowd and don't like being around unruly people. I am not a goony any more I love my family. If they in their mess I can call them on the cell phone. I have a sense of serenity promoting my growth and development of my new life. I have more courage to face life at this age of thirty four like a klump yes I can you already know what it is. God has released twenty two years of oppression off my mind, body, and soul. I got to continue to pray because I am still suffering form being a sinner born.

My parents weren't thinking about me when they did the do for me. I use to be afraid now I am happier then ever. Because God adopted me into a new family bringing me up. As I should not isolated not spiritually dead yes God please work through me. I got a lot of life left I pray you shine through me God so that others. Who's problems great or less then mine they can see just because you give up your life to God doesn't mean it's over your finished. This may not mean anything to most but today it means the world to me. God is good all the time I feel tall as the object in the picture inside with out God in my life I am a stone cold lunatic drunk junky but with God I am somebody.

I am stronger and wiser what I stand for right now is freedom, peace, harmony, security, and goodness. I am willing to make amends and not feel guilty about it. I am going to take care of my earned guilt. This is the key to my life line and the success I will be available for in my life. I do not have to feel guilty about my past it made me who I am now. I am so much stronger now with that behind me that is my wall behind me holding me up. Am I tough well I got some stories and some suggestions in the end you be the judge.

A peace in the inside that no one can take away God has always been right there for me I was ignoring him that is all that was in my past life. The thrill seeking sack chasing party hard life for me is over. Who am I, is cool, calm, and collective I got morale. When I became sober it brought out the best of me. I have real respect that was buried under a lot of B.S. I respect living life today caring about the well being of others and myself. I enjoy the shapes of God's green earth, the beautiful views of large man made buildings. Just things I use to never take the time to recognize I do now. I can't drill this method down any ones throat but I can suggest this program of life.

If you want to know how I got the special quality. The suggestions were given to me freely honestly and very hard core. Keep a open mind stay teachable you will eventually surrender and accept. I am finally okay with regrouping my relationship with me. I learned that it's cool to be alone I am stronger it will not be that way always. Right now I am satisfied with knowing a lot more I am a hot commodity. I have not felt that way about myself since 1991 that's when I thought I was in control of two or more females.

I fooled myself into believing that non-sense that is the very reason why I am lonely now. I am not a dirty-but no more I am happy about that because thinking about this girl that girl drove me crazy. I am only one person and there is to much non-curable things out there this co-dependent doesn't need to be focused on. I already got two ailments Alcohol, and Paranoid Schizophrenia they are enough I am sure that healthy friendship is around the corner. I will be working it right into my sobriety never placing it before my plan of action. I went through hell to get here and I can not afford to allow nothing and no one to have me back in hell.

This celibate think took some getting use to goof things come to those who take care of themselves. I am only doing what a grown man with two young daughters should have been doing all along. I know that I am smart enough to continue to do the next right thing. The goals I set daily are all on the next right thing keeping me focused. My life was unmanageable very disturbed so it is important to treat each day serious. I surrender my will daily accepting things over and over again I am not in control.

Acceptance is the key to my success I am the trigger to my denial my bargains are full of B.S. If I think I have the effort to control or rescue I must think of what got me here. All of my entire life I was always trying to control things knucklehead I was too much of a co-dependent plus alcohol and weed had my mind gone bad. I battled with those drugs in my sins as well as my attitude in trying to run things. I went to war with the world and the drugs twice as stronger when I was angry or scared. Both times I would lose and self medicate wake up in denial like I had won ignoring the issues. Headed strait for self destruction even more I almost lost my mind.

Three years one month and sixteen days later I am finished fighting lions alcohol and negativity gained control of me. Always through my own inviting, and then it started indirectly through others problems. The bottle was my thresh-hold I saw my life flash before my eyes when I held onto that truck. I easily knew I was very unmanageable, spiritually dead, emotionally disturbed and mentally insane. I was out of control I had given up on life once and for all. No more hesitation is allowed in my life I am finally free my journey into the program has been a blessing form God.

Today I have courage that I use to hide so that I could dodge things. No more of that I face my situations head on no regrets they cause resentments and depression. I take pleasure in treating myself and others great. The trigger is me I am the pistol no one put the alcohol in my hands for me but me. I got energy to do other things besides drink and waste time. I am a gentlemen it was hard fought for I am now quote that too. I have had my ups and downs times when no one was around. God came and spoke these words to me Let it go you are forgiven and healed.

I started praying meditating church meetings sharing caring. I learned that prayer confuses the enemy I got victory in my life. I am not scared of living life I know what I got to do to keep what I got. I got a worshipper in me I went from jail back to the same situation that got me locked up in the first place. As time went by trying to work the program I had to leave all the old things in my past there that including that terrible relationship. I was blessed to move on just over come the deceit of that mess. I am on the pursuit to happiness with my life my mind is clear no worry in my heart.

I am freed from allowing myself to suffer under conditions that are not right in relationships. I learned to truthfully stand firm nothing changes if nothing changes my behavior must change. All I like about that relationship was that she listened in the beginning. We had stopped listening to each other long ago I was lying to myself and her for a long time. Forgot the lie and got comfortable nothing was comfortable about it. How could I be comfortable feeling lonely in the inside. I am not that lonely or upset with the ex I am the one who had to change. I told her that I am no prostitute and more I could careless about anyone else being one.

I have been staying celibate knowing that sex is toe be enjoyed not abused. I finally want to discover what is making love because you know that area was wrong too. Everything I am and everything I ever hope to be God is looking inside my heart finding my needs. Only God knows what my future bring long as I strive to survive I can do the right thing. Do I realize the need to slow down and consult my mentors, friends and sponsor before making amends? Have I created more harm in any situation by rushing out to make amends before I was ready? What was the situation?

The majority of my sobriety has been done through the grace of god and writing. I wrote letters to the people I have harmed or vice versa. I will not allow those things to hurt me any more I wrote my oldest sister, my oldest brother and my mom. I have finally finished my mother's letter which was over due. I am living on borrowed time that is the reason I am grateful for the new life. I would be in jail or dead if it wasn't for the goodness of God. I am grateful for my sobriety I tried to make and amend to my so-called friend in Michigan Wade. I was at home for a little while the summer of 2008. I approached the situation powerless the out-come was a total shock to my system.

As I realize that I had been playing with the devil all along. My so-called friends I thought were my friends until the end tried to kill me. We partied one evening I purchased lots of weed and booze. They chipped in whatever they call that any way. I was busy helping get the party in order. I was the maid sort of speaking my friend should have been doing his own things anyway. I was running around while his family members from out of town were handling the weed. I had my weed separate from because it cost a hundred and thirty an ounce. I heard that they crushed up some pills in the weed put it in rotation on me.

No one said a word so-called friends laughed I went coo-coo for at least a year. After that night I never really forgave my so-called friends either until these three years of sobriety kept getting stronger and stronger. My God how stupid I was to think that those were the type of friends I needed to hang with shame on me. I was almost killed I almost killed myself I put myself in that situation never again. Show you what type of friend I was this is the same friend who let me come over and stay when I had gotten put out of my house. Well I stole four of five hundred dollars from my so-called friends.

I wanted to amend it once I told him about that ordeal. My so-called friend instantly said hey my family put that medicine in your weed oh well. Yeah it was total silence on my part I heard somebody laughing. I had my children with me regardless of the fact that is one reason why I must stay focused on my program. I can not take revenge in my own hands making matters worse for myself on top of God's Will for me. So in my new beginning to life I am seeking professional help gratefully. I have shared and chaired meetings every Thursday night in Morganfield, KY.

I was attending AA-meetings frequently keeping in contact with a network of positive people. I always give Honor to God who is the head of my life and the Father of my Lord and Savior Jesus Christ. If you want what I got I got a million suggestions that is all I can do today. Anything else will be uncivilized. I found out if I learned everything there is to know. I still will have questions and will not know it all. Once I got my coin I was still in pain I to keep getting hit over the head with my counselor's lectures. Until I understood that I know now everything I need to know. And if I need answers I will only ask on a need to know basis. The sins will manifest itself in more ways then one.

I will consistently be a student staying teachable to the sickness. I will never know everything I need to know because being a no it all got me drunk. My greatest achievement in life is I learned how to stop being the victim of someone else pain. I learned that people who are involved in being mentored and church and meetings make it like it ort not. The new beginning means stopping the pain controlling my life learning through my mistakes and moving on. No one has ever approached me saying fix this or that you need to. They always say hey men how you doing yada yada.

So it is up to me how I handle my own problems no one can do it for me. If I am scared I was scared all ready no fear because I am the trigger. No one put the drugs and alcohol in my mouth for me. No one told me that doing wrong was not cool. I thought that to myself I made it feel cool. I was a co-dependent to everything in my life before alcohol and drug's my fault. I only suffer even more if I don't try to change it is time for a change. I am changing into a new creation from God I am forever changing. I understand the process of change. I am a butterfly I can fly in my mind more positive I use to play with the saying in the beginning of my sobriety.

If R. Kelly believes he can fly then I can believe that God is going to handle my needs. God's will not my will has accomplished for me in three years what I could never have at all. All I got to do is continue to do exactly what I did to get this close to God. I sought through meditation and prayer to have a conscience contact with God. I am seeking for peace now in my life no more drama and pain it cost to much these days. List of resentments in the way I was still bothered by the incest happening to me. I didn't lay the law down on my oldest brother may God have mercy on his soul as for me. I am great now that is one more chapter to my sobriety.

I was still bothered by some of the traditions my mother laid down for me as a kid. Sorry but I think I got to let them go no need in holding on to fables. i use to resent the example I showed my younger family members. Now I am leading bby example with suggestions. If they want what I got plus I stay with a story to tell a testimony. I am great today there are people in my family that have past away that I could apologize to. I know that has been forgiven already I miss my step dad at times even more being in the process of sobriety.

I know he would enjoy challenging me to stay sober I resent that my mom is in denial about other people that she is allowing herself to fall apart. My mom put her children first I can't or will lose them and everything God's Will supplied for me. I know the principles didn't change all these years people change people. I listened to my mom for many years preach this regular speech. The speech played out for me with the band on Titanic. Mom wants to wake up one day and rich when she is already that in God.

Only God knows what my future may bring I can't think that for a head from fear of what I have already been through I will not make it on my will alone. Can I let these resentments go now? Yes I can let these resentments go now I will not make if in life holding on to all those bags. The guilt that I caused myself is all that I have to worry about you heard me. I have been through hell on earth and what piece of heaven I can pray for while I am alive. All starts at the beginning of everyday God blesses me to wake up and breathe.

I am a miracle I am remarkable I am successful yes I can do anything I put my mind to. I fell in love with alcohol fell out of love with myself. I can rebuild what the alcohol stole from me one day at a time. I didn't start out drinking fifths or gallons. The process took some time and practice I could have been doing anything in the world I chose booze. Huh cause booze doesn't talk back or complain insanity I was ate up all the way just a knucklehead. Well now I got a program I was ate up all the way mistakes I apologize.

If I offended anyone I am sorry keep going on those are things that happen in life. Some things are not that serious I am learning that one day at a time I got peace in my soul. No one can steal that joy from me but me I choose how my day plays out I can either be miserable all day. I can decide to pick myself up pray be happy cheerful and enjoy the new day. All I got is the time before me right now not know other moment so make the best of it God's will and way. Here is where I am to make a list of the people I harmed and how I have harmed them. This is where the letters be placed for my list I must keep it simple. After the process I learned to keep it simple so here are the letters enjoy I feel a million times better. I do not care how they feel it is about my feelings and emotions my health.

Dear, Keiosha and Jasmine this is a wonderful way to express how I feel this year. All the other holiday seasons can't compare to this year. I have the opportunity to say that my two girls are proud of me. Even though we are not together we are in each other's heart. The joy of this time of year is just that the special moments shared. I use to be so lost in a bottle and missed out. I missed out on a lot of holidays being selfish to myself and others. I pray for the days to come for us to be able to share our happiness together. God kept both of my daughters in my life for a reason. I prayed at the beginning of my sobriety for at least one. I knew that I had messed up so much all I could ask for was one.

Please God don't take them away from me I got a second chance to do my best part I can't prove nothing to nobody but God. If I try to prove anything to anyone besides god I will lose my mind again. The Next time I go crazy I will not be coming back from the depths of hell so let's leave that alone. I haven't hit the lottery yet I don't even gamble. I am so honest I feel like Nas said I don't even own illegal cable. Everything about me is legal accept my child-support payment and bad credit.

I never was a hustler because my extra money went on tricking and drinking. Ask me how that's going later I was always a square ask my baby mom. I think it is hip to be square it's the new thirty two inch car rim for me. I'm riding thirty two inches off the ground just playing. So bear with me young ladies I can't wait to see you tow. Hey make up some questions to ask me for Jenga I miss you two to death. This is the first letter from the top to the bottom of my mind and soul to you two.

This isn't one of them old fashioned bottom of my heart letters it's 2010. I originally wrote this in 2008 soon it will be another year we been at the bottom of each other's hearts to long. You tow are the President/CEO of the top functions of my heart. Close your fist Keiosha and Jasmine this is the new faith fight we surviving through. Your closed fist is how big your heart is right now as we speak. Jasmine put the anger down and Keiosha don't wait until you're backed into a corner to express your feelings. Stay calm ladies and when you're asked how much you love me.

Remember to close your fists and say knuckleheads. My fist is bigger so I love you more always trying to do more. Anyway I can go on forever just thought I better be the first man to write my girls a love letter. Before those little guys think they can write better than me. If you think one of them little guys can write good God will be the judge of that plus your mom and I. Lord have mercy on my soul I got to let you two know that I am here for you no matter what you are going through the good and bad.

Before the world as you see it catch your eyes. You two are my babies I love you sorry for ignoring you drinking all the time. Some people are sicker than others know you have forgiven me the past is the past I can't wipe the memories away. I keep seeing your helpless baby faces unable to do anything on your own. I should have stepped up to the plate came into the picture. When your mom told me she was pregnant the first time I went crazy. I went on a fourteen year drinking spree not looking back or caring about nothing but myself.

I lost my ever loving mind Jasmine you got that attitude honest glad you love me. God is good because as much as I held things against people unforgiving. Jasmine I learned a lot from you on forgiveness in three years. I said the party lasted for twelve years of your life. Now you are about to be turning fourteen that was almost all of your life God be the judge leave that alone. Here I am baby the parties over it's all about reality everything is real god got us living on borrowed time and time isn't waiting on no one.

You know something my dad split when I five so therefore I should never have took you two through the misery. I am not perfect you keep on living unless you are God you are going to make some mistakes. I pray I can be there to help you get through it. This is the reality the best words I ever wrote for you two man I am so inspired. Keep up with the good one million five hundred seventy two thousand four hundred and eighty positive minutes. Just continue to seek for peace striving for success if I can do it anyone can I love my sober life. I have three years one month twenty one days sober and I love you so much peace.

This is the best I have ever written in a song from my heart Keiosha Merry Christmas and Happy New Years to you!

(Chorus)

Daddy why are you gone so long/Daddy when are you going to come back home/Daddy why do you got to drink and party/ Daddy When you coming back home/

(Verse-1)

I was living life through binge drinking and anger/You sixteen now for the first thirteen I wasn't there for you/I always had another drunken empty excuse/A deadbeat dad living false fantasies/Keiosha I deserve all the sorrow that came to me/All I ever wanted was for you to run to me/I miss reaching out to pick you up as a baby/I was too drunk and weak you was innocent baby/ If I would have picked you up then/We would have fell down you would never forgave me/All that pretending is for them actors in Hollywood/All those thugs are either dead or in jail/I can't live another day in the life of a alcoholic/There isn't enough inventions to prove how much you mean to me/You are more precious than buildings full of Prada Suede/I want to see you blow candles out on birthday cakes/I want to be in your life when you make good and bad mistakes/There's only so much your mom can do for you/She does so much and stand firm for you/Only a dad can prepare you for the lines and lies/Them guys gone try to sell to you/Your mom strong she fell for the lines and lies too/You don't believe me look at the reflection of you/The truth I'm here forever sober too/I'm learning not to be a foolish fool/If this world were mine I would make another one for you/Keiosha you the new meaning of crazy sexy cool/You got it from your handsome dad and lovely mom/ Merry Christmas and Happy New Years. I love you baby girl peace joy and longsuffering always.

Here's to you Jasmine I love you baby girl the chorus is the same but your verse is your verse.

(Chorus)

Daddy why are you gone so long/Daddy when you going to come back home/Daddy why you got to get your drink and party on/Daddy when will you come back home.

(Verse-1)

Jasmine I think about you all the time/Even when I use to neglect you sipping wine/I remember the lonely times and start crying/Why did I suffer the misery, pain, and shame/Knowing how my dad left me why did I do the same/Your with me in my morning, noon, and nightly prayers/Your part of my tears shed for daily fears/ You're my life story in society I share/I remember your birthdays were my worse days/I use to sip beer and liquor thirsty/Yes I love the life I live today/Jasmine I went from negative to positive and it's all good/I see God's promised sign for the future so divine/I hope you and your mom family doing fine/I love myself today therefore I can love you/I use to be a deadbeat most of our life/I'm straight now you can still hug daddy tight/When I'm with you there's no more lonely roads/Just seeing you takes off the extra load/Sweet heart you a new Brand at Start Bucks Smooth Dark Chocolate Caramel/ Smile you one of the best Benton Harbor Jewels/Take pride in being teachable baby/All leaders got to be good listeners/I'm going to continue to keep rediscovering life/Living recovering from alcohol right/It's what got me this close to you/Now I can truly strive to provide for you/Close your eyes I got a surprise for you let's pray/ God's will gives us whatever we want him to give us/All you got to do is accept, believe and decide. Plus do the next right thing. On top of a billion positive minutes of living/So daddy can ride for you/Until I am old gray and to tired for you/So when I am dead and gone/You will understand I tried for you/It's important for girls to know their dad/I am going to try to be the man there for you when times get harder/You in my heart that's my home/God created that place for you/Through the love I got for you/It's my foundation for us to live for life forever/I'm gearing up in age/Getting as old as I feel/I will still be there for you regardless so just chill/Nothing but the love of God compares to the love I got for you/Nothing compares to you no alcohol no drugs or women/Nothing can come close to this love it's all yours/Whether you like it or not you heard me/Jasmine that's a rap may you have the strength to rejoice in peace joy and long suffering forever/I love you Jasmine Merry Christmas and happy New Years Love your dad Willie X. Pringle written on December 16, 2008 at 10:42 revised October 11, 2010 at 3:37.

(Prayer)

God, the Father of my Lord and savior Jesus. Who is the head of my life. Father you are my light in my darkest moments, my salvation I shall never fear no man. I got the fear of God in me. Forgive me Father for I have sinned against you for years. I didn't know that I had the ability to forgive myself for the molestation and setbacks I was innocent. God is the strength of my life I shall be afraid of nothing. Today I am still suffering falling hard learning from my mistakes. As truth comes to pass I am a grateful recovering alcoholic. I went through hell to get here. This is three years one month and twenty-one days in God's creation. The devil is a liar. I'm praying to God the Father. I use to ask people did they believe in prayer. What's a prayer they'd say prayers change things. Prayers kept me focused on God me and my life of recovery these last three years. Prayers saved me from my desire to drink without fear. I should've been dead in my drinking days. I loved alcohol most when it tried to kill me. I lived a life on a binge deadbeat dad and proud of the fantasy for thirteen years. My children are sixteen and fourteen they call me daily to see what's happening. Prayers help me die out of the old me. Prayers kept me alive in 1995/When those bullets cut through the air/Prayers of the righteous help me say I been shot at never shot/I should've fell then and prayed instantly/Prayers are spiritual medicine from the power of Jesus/It heals wounds internal and externally/Ask some people spiritually fit and the people still suffering/I'll keep it on me in my sobriety I still suffer daily/In my drinking days I was spiritually dead in my community/I had a co-dependency to misery/Living isolated like cold dead people/Nothing but the hype of the in-crowd kept me going/Surrendering helped me realize power in prayers/All I had to do was close my eyes/Put my hands together/Bow my head/ Ask Jesus to keep me on the right path/Keep me out of jails, and institutions/Before the next step be death/Please God protect our children/Save our suffering families Dear God here we are/I repent my sins forgive me for the mistakes/The pain runs deep/ Forgive all the disrespectful nights I made moms cry/The running wild in the streets/God forgive me here I am/I pray to God daily to strengthen me/I did harmful things in my past/I need thy will to be done to wipe it away/That old way will never happen again/Prayer takes the pain away/I use to couldn't speak on it/Thank God for blessing my writing I got a gift I can use it/I use to couldn't sleep homie/Now it's strengthening my weaknesses/I can take the pain with the losses/Praying more carrying my cross today/I'm living on borrowed time forgive me Father/I am a sinner born sinning got me sober/Where I am today was by the grace and mercy of God/I got a testimony and a prayer today I never would have made it without Jesus/Praying prayer hurt or not/I thank God for showing me he cares/I will not shut-down my capabilities ever again man-up to my problems sending prayers in the air/I use to live like a free loader/ Where I'm at is my home/Now I'm down on my knees praying daily/Back to back moaning and groaning/My life is much better the best ever/I can live peacefully, joyous through long-suffering/ Whether walking or riding a bike/Rain, sleet, or snow, still grateful/ Life keeps moving on and on/God has been there through all my thick and thin/I been sitting back thinking/How my mom battled between two alcoholics/May my step dad rest in peace/Proves she was just as sick but getting better/I got a three page resume living a lie for years/I couldn't keep a nine to five wondering why/I was paranoid on the streets of homicidal booze/Schizophrenic living for the in-crowd was completely suicide/It took thirty one years to get three years and one month sober/I surrendered my will to God's will/God sent me to another way again literally/So I could admit accept and decide/Another way of life was the way for me/So just call me a case of can't get right getting it right/It took twenty-seven years to get three years and twenty two days sober. You can hate me so I love you anyway. My story is unchangeable from family to family. You can live trying to live or die trying to live either way you got to do it living that is peace.

(Letter to my older brother)

Another letter written during my up rise toward salvation and sobriety to my older brother on my mom side I love you big brother. Dear, Leaon I would like to start out by saying hello to the family. Sorry we have never met sure you all have heard a lot about us. If not shame on Leaon one day we will get the opportunity. I pray we meet before my niece graduates from college. It has been twenty four years you just will not show your face. You starting to have more excuses then Reshonda when she threw herself down the stairs. Maybe you call yourself disowning us for whatever reason. Well let's see what has changed since I last saw you. You went to the army to be all that you could be.

So did I how did that work out for you. I sis the left right left BDU's and boots yes Drill Sgt. No Drill Sgt. You got married are you happy is she how is that going. My marriage lasted about eight months happily the best eight months I could afford. After eight months it was murder she wrote. We both got children they have never seen each other if I didn't have pictures of you. I wouldn't know how you look we are not getting any younger. Leaon You missed so many holidays it's only right to work on my new life. I thought this was being rude for this time of year. If it had not been for the molesting I wouldn't even consider you family anyway. See that's where God's will and my new way of living kick in.

I am delivered from that way of thinking it took three years one month and twenty one days. I finally can say that proud of who I am today. Regardless of my past that entire trauma I don't have to allow that stuff to haunt me. Another way means my behavior has changed the graphics in details are to vulgar. If you are reading this in front of your family great my children know about it Mr. Family Guy. Tell the truth and shame the devil. I been through hell and back in my life fighting running away from everything. I am sober now all that stuff that took place in Benton Harbor, MI at 1725 Council Dr. in Berrien Homes stays. I use to smoke weed and drink for years thinking about the day I laid eyes on you face to face. The outcome would be on some Cane-Abel. Horrible I even had a pack of hungry werewolves to eat the case.

I know good and well you wouldn't want no smoke. After it was said and done. I finally learned that I can't think like that about no one if I am going to get better. I got the Benton harbor Township Sheriff's dept to come to Grandpa house on 1314 Rose Ave. Back in 1996 or 1997 you remember that they had a certified letter from Wichita Kansas Prison. Telling me that I had to stop writing you my literature was causing an outbreak in the prison. What's understood doesn't need to be explained the hell it don't I refuse to take this burden I lived with into 2009. When I first wrote this letter it is now revised in 2010 for the primary purpose to show people how to forgive.

Things happen for a reason meanness is as ancient as any evil deeds that are performed. You left Benton Harbor, MI full of anger and rage wanting to hurt some people. Look you already did that right whoever them people was that jumped you they wasn't your family. I can't call it that's not my problem it is the molesting anyway I do remember how can I forget. I know that Christopher Columbus don't discover America in 1492. I discovered America in 1725 a great many years might I add. I don't regret it I will not be going back to that mind state no time soon. If I do snap there will be consequences and a whole lot of repercussions.

This speech is coming straight from the heart of the love I gained through the grace of God. My actions are guided by the story you know too well from the bible the book of "Joseph." Joseph's parents were proud parents when Joseph was born remind me just how mine was for me. They were in there old age you know they had a right to be proud old-timers. Joseph had favor with his dad because out of all the children already in the family. Joseph was the baby boy it was a lot of them Joseph got all the attention. Just like I did when I was a born needless to say it wasn't twelve of us. I wasn't a bad child in the beginning it was only three children at my house.

I can remember mom giving me the undivided attention. It was a short lived fame but I had it you know Joseph had a calmness to his attitude at a young age. So did I so did I right now Leaon I am claiming my victory. In this letter to you right along with Joseph. I grew up a dreamer almost lost out on seeing them dreams through to the end. Joseph had dreams of being in rulership over his eleven other older brothers. Think if I would have said back when I was eight or nine. I am going to have leadership over you and Reshonda you would have probably hit me in the stomach or something. Now in no way would you have believed that story or dream. Just like Joseph's brothers they really hated him because Joseph was the favorite child.

I was the favorite child I thought I was special. Joseph's brothers tried to kill him and sold him into slavery. Now with that being said I look at my life and the things that happened. My brother and sister mistreated me betrayed me sexually. God took Joseph through it so that the story could be of some sort of inspiration to the people in Egypt. Well it has my vote no you and Reshonda didn't sell me to slavery or try to kill me. What did happen as a result of the molestation. I shut down my ability to feel emotions love and avoid pain. I grew a very weak co-dependent to things because of that mess. You know meanness is ancient but God has all power everlasting to everlasting.

You feel me Leaon I don't know all about that sexual activity played out with you and Reshonda. I do know that something had to have been going on between you two. The devil is a liar what had happened was you and her both knew I would tell . So you and her tried to keep me from knowing so much for that idea. I am grateful I didn't become gay God made Adam and Eve. If God made anything better than a women he kept it to himself some people are sicker than others. I am grateful that those days of miserable suffering is behind me. I lived shut down from the world for twenty seven years and at age twenty two they called my breakdown (Paranoid Schizophrenia).

The miracle is that my mind was stronger at the age of eight or nine then it is now. I am thirty four years old. I have three years one month and twenty one days sober it was times when my mind couldn't take the stress. I never wanted to kill myself but unlike my dad actually doing it. I thought about it yeah I Thank God how all this pan-out. Know he meant every word that's why I kept it in for this long. I am not apologizing no more Happy Holiday Christmas is daily. Thinking about that stuff had me hurting Harold my step dad all the time. We fought trying to overcome the pain still hurting each other. Nothing worked you'll never guess until I stopped everything and gave my will to God. I told on Reshonda back then and it didn't help mom just put her out quick.

I just told mom about what went on with you in Sept-Oct 2008. Regardless we still family and part of family is getting over any hurdle takes unity together. If not oh well denial almost killed me God get fed up with my foolishness he prevailed. We are all going to die trying to do something as for me. I choose to die trying to live sober. Look it is not like you've been making a great effort to see your family anyway. My tears are all dried up on that tip now mom on the other hand. She may still have some left for you not coming around I think twenty four years is long enough for a secret to be kept it's out the bag peace. People change principles remain I will not start talking in another way code.

I know you probably saying man I am still remembering that stuff. I am alive hell yeah I remember it an I probably will for the rest of my life. Thanks no matter how big you get or think you are that haunts me I was always sensitive. I don't wish any bad things on you like I use to lets just keep it that way. I know longer threat you like a gift horse any more. The Trojan horse was sent as a gift full of warriors into the camp. As soon as night fell they came out to attack God is fighting my battle I got fifty thousand pounds of pressure lifted off my shoulders. I refuse to take resentments to the grave or into the next year. So if it be God's will and I think of some more things that eat my lunch better believe before it is all said and done.

I will handle it you don't have to front it can't be changed. My pretending days are over all the acting is for them actors in Hollywood. The courage I got Leaon to get this wow I can suggest just a few things. I can't tell you about your life to each person their own way. You know God knows all he see everything even when you think people can't he can. I grew up exacting to much faith in people I grew up use to exacting that's what I call it (Exacting) expecting too much out of other people. I don't know about you I went through hell to get sober. I am scared of those people who have never suffered hard times. You may be one of them form the ghetto but act like you was raised in the suburbs.

Well I thank God everyday for allowing me to be self sufficient in Jesus name three years one month and twenty one days sober. If I never would have fell down and hurt myself or went through hell living on earth or made it through any unbearable mishaps. I would not be sober right now able to tell my entire story I would not be writing you nothing right now you would not even know if I was alive or not. God is my life line I can call him up any time all day and he is always there to hear my cry. Leaon this is for you how I love Jesus he loved me before the molestation took place. There were ten men in the bible with leprosy they were standing in a distance. Because as tradition had it back then leprosy was very catching.

People who had it back then had to call out before you crossed their path condemned stay away. They saw Jesus in a distance and called out to him save me heal me. Jesus said go to the Priest and show him thy self approved to the priest. The priest had to examine the bodies of the men with Leprosy to see if they were healed before they could go back to society. The ten men went only one came back praying and magnifying the Lord for what he done. You know what happened the other nine men they said they were just going to take Jesus word for it. Instead of being obedient well that one guy had enough faith to be healed and he was right. We can say we'll go back in time erase it nope it's just like the torn in Paul side.

I am not preaching just doing what I have been instructed to do with my sobriety. Jesus left that thorn in Paul's side for a reason Paul got all his blessings healed he may have forgotten where he came from feel me. If god were to heal you of everything that ever happened to you would you need God you need to bow down and pray daily this is where your prayers take shape. You don't hear me. It could have been worse for all of us. People have been through much more or less they are not alive to talk to their older brother like me to even have a conversation. If you mad you were already mad I am not mad at you.

The past is the past your past is your past mine is mine. I will not brush any of my dirt from my past on your porch anymore. I will not go around like it didn't happen anymore either. I can carry the message to those who still suffer that gives me peace. God's will is the power that guided me to get up out of living life as a alcoholic deadbeat dad. If you willing to surrender your will to God's will you got it. You heard bishop Howard Thomas preach before don't act brand new. Leaon remember bad weather tornadoes hurricanes etc were created by God too he sent them. Bad storms are symbols for those who know to repent not try to figure out why God destroyed this or that.

Jesus doesn't do nothing for no reason everything has a purpose pray. You are a miracle unless you know somebody breathing into dirt creating people let me know if you do. Regardless of what the circumstances we still family. There is always someone going through or been through just as worse. So don't think I am ridiculing or pointing the finger at you I am just at the place in my life. I got sick and tired of the shackles of misery being the issue. My down falls were not justified good enough. I am somebody blessed to be alive. I deserve to live out the rest of my life as God intends.

People say I am Mr. Preacher all AA just can relate to trauma to help people get past their hurt that's all. Nope I am giving inspiration back to the community of a dying breed of generational cursed people. How I got it was one day at a time this is for my home boy Russell (RAW) an uncut Rigorous angrily Wildly ambition of a writer ever seen or read. Just saying sorry alone is not repair enough for the damage it has caused. Sorry didn't do the damage and I've found out that sorry I may not have been sorry people who are sorry don't do hurtful things out of spite. I could've cared less and if I did not have God in my life now I wouldn't be writing this now believe me sorry is unacceptable. Why is only changing my behavior not sufficient to repair the damage I have caused?

I would be like a dry drunk without changing everything about my outlook on life in many ways there would be no change. My actions behind the behavioral change must be from the heart and of my own doing not for the sake of anyone else or it will not be genuine. We call it sincere from the heart rigorously tapping into the personality that makes me enjoy stealing even though it is bad. My mind my train of thought has to be reorganized so that all the terror is in another way. Doing wrong things has become easy things to so easy that normal living for me seemed lame. Now that it is hip to be square I enjoy one day at a time.

I am not a thrill seeker living on the edge I don't run to the gun fights just like when I use to be out here doing wrong. I use to avoid all things that people would say were right for me. If my mom said anything to me in my drinking days like you know green will bring you wealth. Hey I wouldn't be wealthy because I didn't want to hear that stuff. I am stronger at owning up to my wrong doings I am excited that when I make a mistake or hurt someone I am able to really say I apologize. I remember a time when I wouldn't even care forget the results. Mainly because of what happened to me in my past it didn't kill me. I am only stronger I got remarkable courage now never was a killer I would have been killed someone or myself.

Those extension cords whipped me into shape now I am looking eye to eye with my parents. Both of them in they own way are apologizing but nothing will be sufficient enough for me accept having the opportunity to whip them back with a extension cord or dog leash. I don't think that is a healthy part of my pursuit to another way. Help me design a way to pay back that terror haha. I am just as addicted to doing right as I was to doing wrong. The bible says in all thy ways acknowledge him and he shall direct thy paths. I am great not every day but working on it. I can live sober because it will never be as bad as it was when I was drinking.

I never want to live that way ever please God if I ever get to that point again body slam me. Do I have financial amends that I don't want to make? Right now I have been going through this part of my life for a reason. Plenty of times I was working a promising job great benefits factory etc. Well I use to be in love with alcohol those jobs meant everything to the people around me. They didn't mean nothing to me I use to be hot headed and would walk off jobs, go to work drunk or hung over leave never return. I worked for the city in Indianapolis must been some awesome job because I skipped the other ones. Right now all jobs are blessings for people that have them all my job history was a lie. My resume said exactly what they were looking for on that paper.

My way of living is rigorous honesty. I got two daughters that I am trying to teach by leading and it is not kind for me to lie. So my cousin who works in the Human Resources at the Citizens Gas got me the job. I left weed alone years ago my drinking then was to the roof and beyond. Well my birthday in 2004 I was working through manpower at Citizens Gas making thirteen dollars a hour. Supposed to have been ninety days hired into the company took seven months. Yes my drinking was a problem one of my crew members told on me. The plant manager accused me of drinking on the job which was a lie.

I never drink on the job because I drank too much at home away from work the plant manager told me I was fired and I said no I am not Manpower Hired me and Manpower will fire me. I stayed working it was a big political thing anyway because all of the temporary workers were black. I used it to the best of my ability without letting on that she was my cousin. We had a snitch in the group of us four workers I worked with Ed. Sanders. I said that because I drank enough to go to work tore up every day and not bring it to work. I was a knucklehead not stupid one day I was at work super hung over.

I couldn't stay awake in front of the boss the same guy who tried to fire me. Anyway I way the only person who fit in the steam drums in the boiler rooms. Yeah he made me do extra work but in the end he respected me for standing up for myself. He recommended that I did not get picked to go any further into the company. But I had favor in the Human Resources my cousin told me a few weeks before so I already had the heads up. The guy who told about the drinking on the job was laughing for sure. His name Terry well anyways he was at the big plant before me. I got there he had his head all down I still didn't care too much. Even all that butt kissing he did didn't work he couldn't handle the truth.

Now my financial problems are my fault my bad credit and poor judgment on paying bills on time have reflected what type of person I was in my drinking day. I created them so I must pay them off soon as I get my career going. I have goals as for how to overcome my bad credit problems overdue bills. I got thirty six months of funding to go to school. Okay I will work at a job close to my career study then I will get a print out of my credit report. As a drastic goal in thirty six months I don't care if I work a four hour a week job I will start paying those bills off. During the process of elimination I will not stack any more bills on myself. Just one way for me to stay focused on my goals successfully.

I have been changed from the inside out not seeking that big pay day. I know how to survive off what I have and enjoy it. I had to learn how to do that I use to steal sell anything from sex to lies to get what I thought I needed. I got my chip from another way in my wallet all the time. I went through hell to get that chip man and I am rich in sobriety. I couldn't buy this feeling with all the money in the world. I would probably lose it if I could buy it somewhere else. I thank God I surrendered when I did no telling where I would be today. Oh yeah I thought I was going to have a problem with a friend everything is cool experience strength and hope is for real.

Oh yeah anybody put they hands on me I am calling the police now I got witnesses to back me up. I will not just stand for a beat down either. If warning the police called doesn't scare them after they've done already hit me upside the head. I got to defend myself god know s where my heart is the next right thing. Do I owe amends to people who have harmed me? TO be honest I dove head first into my sobriety ready to conquer the madness. I didn't know where to start at first until I wrote that autobiography. I hit a stepping stone to delve into bit by bit until I found something. I have been forgiven for all the harm I have caused whether people believe it or not.

I can't worry about how other people feel I know where my life stands. Sobriety for me is in the hands of God for all them do gooders that I harmed or harmed me. I am healed saved it is my past I must move on like the end of all my steps say. Move on through the good and the bad it will always materialize if I work for it. I am a survivor I can't give up or back down from none of my fears. Fear means doubt then I would be doubt God and that is not cool I got faith. I know that I would be drunk buy the end of every evening in my sin.

I got more faith in God in my life when it is time for me to have companionship in my life. I am no longer a dirty butt so I will be ready healthy and very influential. My sobriety has millions of suggestions and advice if people don't mind listening to and old alcoholic. I use to listen to way worse kind people in my drinking days. Mainly I had to get out of listening to myself and hear what positive people had to say to me. How in the world could I have expected any one to do what I wanted as messed up as I were I am a positive person. I enjoy who I am I rediscovered the meaning of living through my sobriety.

My counselor Jennifer is one heck of a pusher she pushed me right on through the golden gate way. Although yeah she says it all the time her job is so much easier when the person is ready and willing to make a change. Willing to change who I am most people want to change but don't know how it's like buying new car, clothes, house, etc. When you go check it out everything better work you say it to yourself. The outside looks superb check it all out then purchase it. Relax and start finding things wrong with your judgment you did it. Huh that is life right there only can work each day God grant you the serenity to accept the things you can't change.

Change your mind then decide to change it again only you can prevent forest fires. (A letter to Mom)Dear mom, the last three years one month and twenty one days have been the best days of my life. I went through hell on earth to get where I am comfortable in my own skin. I truly am happy of who I am today this very moment. I am not trying to, or will I ever be able to live up to any expectations other people have for me. I am all that I am who I am only God know. All that I am and what I will become is up to God also. Nevertheless this letter is about how I use to live under you leadership. Charity starts at home and then spread abroad I didn't steal from outside the home first then start stealing from other outsides the home. I saw people in my household doing all kinds of things from you all the way down to me.

I learned all about that all too well growing up a Pringle. The decisions you made every minute of your life were supposed to shape the person I was to become. So you hoped Thank God for Jesus he had other plans for me in my life. This life I am living isn't about right or wrong. You or me there I go trying to make up for just getting smart. Anyway I was a co-dependent to everything my little eyes laid sight to for a long time. I was like the water boy momma said you even told me you got pregnant by eating salad. Life isn't fair and people don't act right so I came to learn. Now I am a firm believer please don't I almost forgot I eliminated the middle man by typing this letter. I was just about to say if you got one of your younger daughters reading this great.

Just one more point in this drama filled family you always putting irresponsible children in charge of grownups. I went through hell once I will not go back so that's why I am freely writing this letter. I am not in jail or nothing it is just time for you to forgive yourself for some of the madness and move on. On august 20, 2007 I surrendered admitted accepted came to believe and decide. Once and for all I was sick and tired of living behind the image of unhealthy companionships. I was raised into drama maybe you had my best interest at heart. You beat and raised all your three oldest out of five children until we got older. None of the chastening worked for me no matter how bad that sounds.

Until I opened up my mind and heart to seek God for myself I would still be miserable a knucklehead running away from all my problems. Mom I ran –away stole fought in a gang drank and sold a little drugs. I loved school it was a escape for me if you are ever wondering. I could disappear from the Pringles in any lesson at any time Thank God. I gained a skill in writing God's gift to me I shall not abuse it. Oh how bad you just don't know how much I want to. My sobriety doesn't host revenge mom I don't know where all the anger came from you holding inside but I didn't do it. I pretended to all my life to be slow or retarded but when God placed me in that psych-ward. I was around people that really needed help they were not acting I got scared to death. My life was unmanageable then I just couldn't let go of the booze.

You know something I accepted the fact right in that psych ward that maybe people were right I was not crazy. Just a little touched but not crazy sure you make mistakes but not near as bad as to send yourself through the torment and humiliation. I still went crazy mom you always wanted to know why I got out of that condition healthy and went back to the streets. Blue Mondays I loved the way drinking appeared to me everybody in the family made it look so enjoyable. All the bar-be-que party social gatherings it was on and popping. I was attracted to the wrong way of living for so long nothing made sense. Until I could see that the party I was in lasted way to long. I was either going to die with a beer in my hand or get myself together.

I lost my mind in the whole meaning of living and didn't never know how to be in a relationship. My parents' great idea of being in a good relationship was dealing with people they were tired of but just because. I couldn't ask you two knuckleheads about life. You were on two different wave lengths. I had to find out the hard way sure enough I finally tapped out living life a maniac. I was holding on to the back of a speeding Expedition in 2007. God actually had enough time to show me how unmanageable my life had become. This time deep down I knew if I didn't get any help I would be in jail for ever or dead. I am not lying it is true after all those fights with Harold, baby mom, and people on the streets. I was in many brushes with death I still hopped on the back of that truck. As if I was in total control of things.

I found the answer at that point that I was crazy now I got the key to happiness. God has accepted me into his kingdom I never wanted to be as rude as the rest of your children. You should have put the responsibility of watching your children in the hands of a mature grown up instead of children. I will not go another day thinking that you are always going to compare me to other children. Plus Harold's alcoholism is his problem not mine or yours you are a great enabler. You love us to death regardless of how much you see something killing us you supply it. No one is perfect and until you learn what it is you will never know. I have been learning about alcoholism for three years mom you are as sick as we are to put up with all of us and our mess.

I will not name or label anymore items of your children we're all got problems. I am not in denial about mine they maybe think I don't care how people think or feel about me. This includes you if you think I act like my big sister or brother so be it. You need to get out more who did you expect me to act like you left me with them all the time. See one thing is for sure you had to many things in front of God that as a new Christian made it difficult for you. Yeah you were a single parent mother you put all your thoughts and feelings into your children. We let you down over and over again people change principles do not. Thirty nine years Bishop Thomas has been preaching the word of God you know it.

The word has remained forever the same the concepts that you and my dad thought home were your own concepts. Mom God's will was not for you to be out there running up behind us putting yourself in danger. I guess you figured you chased them may as well chase me. I pray that God gives me the power to stand firm in his word so if my two daughters start acting out I will not lose any rest. I can rest in the word of God. Mom you did your God given best in raising five children we are grown. Now you did all that you could we made it. You know every story every wound every memory. My whole life happiness use to be wrapped up in your single moment don't you get it. I am thirty four years old you let your life pass on by putting us first.

Holding things over my head like bailing me out I can't pay you back for all that you ever done. What is in the heart if it was not in your heart you should have never done them. Just forgive yourself I forgive myself now that I know the truth. You couldn't and will not be there all the time to rescue me I must learn to defend myself that is why I am telling you. Mom forgive yourself then God can forgive if you have then things will be alright. One day we all will be a family again God's will for us maybe our family style is powerful enough to show people who still suffer that even we can make it. I am still alive still suffering if not today god's will I will know how to handle anything life has to throw my way. I think it is a shame for our family to still be alive and go around day to year upset. Why it's out of our hands if you mad you were mad already.

I think we have learned how to let go of hard hearts harboring resentments. Those types of things will make you fall short of the kingdom open up your heart and let the sunshine in. I am still alive for a reason I know God is real. I am at a place in my life I never thought possible single happy about it now getting answers to things that use to bother me. I got sober and commend you for putting up with all of family's addictions. Remember you are just as sick as we are mom you know what my fear was that on day. I would stand up in a empty room you would be thinking that I acted or did something because your other children were like he is who he is myself.

I use to always want you there with me like when that guy broke into our apartment and stole our Christmas presents. I was young enough to remember he bust the back window and came in and took all our presents and cooked oat-meal and made hot dogs. Maybe because from the food he took we would have known who he was fiend. I got God in my life whenever wherever I am you are there to in my heart. How can I ever forget mom I was a special child I had four parents to experiment with. I am thinking better then I use to way better I pray for everything worry about nothing. Mom you are part of my past present and each prayer set forward God's will.

My future is totally up to God you did a great job with some mistakes in raising me oh boy did you. Mom strap on your prayer boots lace them up its faith fighting time. First forgive yourself right now you couldn't be every place that job is for God we are here for reason let's pray about it. O let's all of us go to church and act a fool like we did at home you too. Seeking for peace mom when I came out the womb did you right away know that I was going to be handsome or did it take you a few glances. Peace your sober son Willie X. Pringle.

"This represents the forgiveness in a total package to teach my children. My ex-wife and I never got along but my new way of living has made us adults plus she ahs five children mine the oldest and I love them as well as mine true love for all God's children ans people oh yeah it was during the Obama Champaign and Congress Rep Stabinow posed with us."

Dream Come True
Michigan Native Henderson Resident
Prize-Winning Playwright
Second runner-up

I know a thing or two about hard times, but there's grace and mercy from God to heal a nation. I am a resident of Henderson, KY and a native from Michigan. I have drawn on my experiences in life to write a play so profound if has nothing to do with my life. The play is strictly brand new entertainment for this day and time. I know all too well how people turn their lives around and use the mess to create a story. I wasn't that popular before I decided to change and I am not that popular now. A second runner up winner in the 2010 play writing contest hosted by the Black Gospel Play Association out of Nashville, TN.

The Play is titled "Where We Come From" the original was "Where We Came From" the primary message is to show people especially children that they can have a voice in changing abusive situations they might find themselves in. "It's a positive message alcohol and drugs will ruin your life. I am a full time college student at Henderson community college. My style of writing is different from what the Henderson Community College has witnessed they couldn't relate to my material. Nevertheless God blessed me to find some people who knew exactly what my writing needed. When I presented the play to the performing arts department on campus at the HCC they didn't understand what I wanted them to do. I don't hold any hard feelings toward them only God can see the future for this idea. The play ended up being exactly what God intended it to be National.

I have always written poetry, songs, essays, letters, cards and other things, but this was my first time for writing a play. I found the information about the contest run by the Nashville based organization on the internet and decided to give it a try. I really want to bring the powerful message to the mainstream. The view of this drama filled play is written from the 8-12 year old perspective. "It really stuck out to me," the mission statement at our church-For all to encounter God and grow into lives of service and fulfillment. We can join in the fight to uplift and inspire our nation through messages in the medium of theatre.

This opportunity is priceless to be at such a level in my life. I am saved sober and focused. I can explain how God restored my mind back to sanity. I was given a second chance after they diagnosed me with being a paranoid schizophrenic. I can explain the process that God has designed for all to be sober-minded receiving the promises he created for us. I am a living miracle of the true divine order and oracles of God by being a responsible dad. I am no longer a dead beat irresponsible dad I love my life. Almost four years ago you wouldn't catch me saying anything positive. God has turned my life around and I pray that I can make an impact on people and children to choose life. I decided that even if I didn't win, at least I had tried it.

You know it took God 31 years to open my eyes nothing happens over night it is all a process. I am in the process the play is set around families struggling with issues of trust, self-respect, and problems with alcohol and drugs. My writing style is very true to life making it a play for centuries to come a revolution. I thank God for the correction coming in the form of water in Tennessee.

The play writing deadline was pushed back a couple of months by the spring floods that covered Nashville, which opened up a door of opportunity for me to finish the my work.

"I wrapped it up better than any Christmas present I ever gave and sent it in." It was six days later I was notified that my play had been selected as a winner. After a period in my life from 7-31 years of age I dealt with my own self destruction like a Egyptian in the wilderness. I have taken a vow to be sober-minded and see my writing as a way to pass along the importance of such a choice. One of the elements of the play is Gospel music I wrote for it. The music includes the Theme song "Turn Your Life Around." I got to acknowledge my good friend Min. Frank Cole he has a few songs he wrote on the sound track also. "Before I got saved I was in a group called 4-life Click we were rappers. We performed this song in the studio I recall, my church up bringing came out in the booth. I presented my verses so profoundly that my group gave me the song and told me to use that for my solo hit.

Now it gets straight to the point for me I give credit to my church family Love Temple Church of God In Christ. (Including Supt. Harlan Armstead, and wife Evang. Missionary Sharon Armstead). I am grateful for being allowed to be a part of their church family grafted in as God has designed it to be. I am grateful for how they are helping to shape and mold me into a productive citizen. "I had a real life changing experience." I was homeless for six months out of my life to become independent. I was praying and asking God to lead me into independence my route was homelessness. I use to think that homelessness was beneath me in my drinking day. Peace to the Harbor House may God Bless each and every one of you.

I have to also credit my counselors at Another-Way in Morganfield KY for allowing me to have a second chance to get right. "They showed me that it takes a tribe to raise one child. I have to listen to somebody every place I go like it or not." I am not exactly sure what will happen in my future only God knows I pray that I can get help to produce this play and tell my story so that people can truly be healed and set free. My life story began with being molested at a young age. I shut-down for 25 years or more abusing myself my older sister and brother were the enemy. I didn't like them and we had ugly relationships mainly never talking. As I began to grow into being sober we have all forgiven ourselves and moved on so powerful for people to know forgiveness has to start inside. We are all doing well today and placing the past in the past is the best thing that ever happened to us. We were all young and experimenting and things got out of hand.

As a family we can bring this powerful message just like the sibling rivalry with Joseph but in the end who did God make the leader. I know the play needs to be produced but I already feel like a dream Has Come True.

Scene 1 Where We Come From

> Man-Man/Duke
>> Beating up Sylvester
> Man-Man/Duke
>> Yelling Where My Money At

Sylvester	Calm Down, Calm Down
Man-Man	Crime doesn't have lay-a-way plans
	Sylvester you better pay up or become a victim
Jeena	Why don't you just pay them vester haven't you lost enough already
Duke	Every time I ask you for my money you think it's a joke
Sylvester	Oh you two are some real thugs. Is that it!!
Man-Man	Hold him hold him

> Man-Man/Duke
>> Still beating on Sylvester

Jeena	Do you care about our life Sylvester they will kill us
Man-Man	Pay up or get done in/It's cut throat around here
Sylvester	You chump change wannabe thugs huh
Man-Man	You need to be worried about C-Luv
Duke	Yeah making sure C-luv doesn't find out about this deal of ours I don't think he will be pleased
Man-Man	If he is anything like his parents (Snitches) he's probably trying to tell on someone right now. Ha Ha Ha

163

Duke	Matter fact I can hear him trying to tell on somebody right now
Sylvester	We got witness protection/Real thugs don't drop murder weapons
Man-Man	(Snatch-Money)
Jeena	We got each other Sylvester/What yall got
Duke	Right now Chump change/
	Man-Man/Duke

Mocking Sylvester and Jeena (We got each other) Witness protection

Man-Man/Duke

Still laughing loud yelling Thanks for the chump change

If you tell C-Luv it will be ugly for him keep him quiet.

Det. Leslie

Well, Well, Well

Sylvester

What is it now

Det. Leslie

If it aint slick 50, Jeena

Sylvester

Don't you got crooks to catch

Det. Leslie

You, two are just the crooks I need to see

Jeena

Chase them two that just did this to Vester

Det. Leslie

Yeah your problems seem to be catching up with you

Sylvester

you see what I'm going through it aint right

Jeena

Vester baby you alright here's a band-aid be still there suga

Sylvester

Ouuch!

Det. Leslie

We have evidence about Mrs. Scotts murder that is pointing toward you two huh!

Jeena

What on earth!!! Please

Sylvester

Man please we been informants for 36 years this isn't new to us do your job

Jeena

You police don't have anything better to do then pick pick pick somebody gone get hurt

Sylvester

All of a sudden we turned killer after all we have done for the precinct that's right baby somebody gone get hurt feelings or something

Jeena

Excuse me Mr. Officer Mr. Boss Man

Det. Leslie

Huh   Detective now please come with us (Thank You)

Jeena

We are entitled to witness protection MR. Cake Boss

Sylvester

Hilarious the young Man finally received a promotion hear that Jeena

Jeena

Three years on the division Ha Ha Ha Oh my God! He's still a baby

Sylvester

C-luv can solve more cases then him we need some coffee and donuts please sir

Jeena

McDonald's keep fresh coffee I saw the pots full on the way up here

Det. Leslie

I see we have two comedians the evidence pending needs your cooperation

Sylvester

You should've stayed in school young man or is it Detective

Det. Leslie

You two are going to suffer the consequences not me

Jeena

We need our phone call and visit to show you how it works

Sylvester

Mr. Detective you do whatever it takes to get my son in here to visit us ASAP that means right now

Jeena

We need (15-min) with C-Luv he's smart enough to know when something is wrong

Sylvester

If we are not at the spot by the time C-Luv gets there he will know there is a major problem

Jeena/Vester

Well get to moving did you hear us chop chop

Sylvester

You think it is a joke and wonder why you can't catch criminals

Jeena

Get a move on it cause in about (20-min) the neighborhood will be a war-zone

Sylvester

The neighborhood will only be fit to battle like in Iraq/Iran Hurry

Jeena

Enough talking Vester let them do their jobs. Now go get C-Luv with all this technology wires yall still can't find nothing and nobody

Det. Leslie

That's why they made (Snitches) like you two Ha Ha Ha

Sylvester

Your waisting Government money and time pitiful out right pitiful

Jeena

You couldn't find a clue if you were a winner on Wheel of Fortune. I bet you want to buy a vowel. Just find C-luv!!

Doctor

Let us pray because for the many women who come into this hospital battered and bruised but leave a corpse.

Felicia

I guess I can give God some time Oh God it's been a long time since I've talked to you

Doctor

Many women leave this hospital some survive many end up in the morgue Let us pray that you be that inspiration for women who need help

Felicia

I got to start over Jesus please help us we need your guidance to find a better way

Doctor

Have your way In the Name of Jesus we know you're in control of that which we may not get another chance ever to correct the wrong we are striving for peace

Felicia

Create in me a new being show me Who I am, O Lord God, and what is my purpose in my life and in my family

Doctor

Help us to grow in the grace of Thy Will have mercy on our Souls have mercy on our souls

Felicia

Dear God I need you to Heal all our sorrow and help us to maintain in life through the good and bad times

Doctor

We can only endure so much alone in these perilous times Help us O Lord to come together in times like these we need a saviour

Felicia

Help me heal us deliver us bless our families bless the churches the community

Doctor

Help us Lord, Help our families through sickness, abuse, and health bring us together as one in your name Christ Jesus Amen!!

End of Scene-1
Parent's Disown Felicia ©

Kay-Kay
(Mistakes Felicia for dead)
Kay-Kay She makes a scene

Kay-Kay

Oh God no don't take my daughter, O not my daughter please don't take her away from me

Victor

Kay-Kay Get yourself together stop acting up Felicia over there get up you didn't scream that much when you was in labor with her

Doctor

I appreciate your family participating in the extended outreach counseling

Victor

What's that you say huh I'm the Dad say that again Doc

Doctor

The extended outreach program is counseling for the victim

Felicia

Can I be excused it's time to go I'm tired and hungry

Victor

Thank God, Felicia you need to utilize all that they have to offer like it or not

Kay-Kay

Yeah cause You the one that have to live with the abuse not us

Doctor

You have to realize Felicia that abuse has occurred in front of your children

Kay-Kay

Have you lost your mind we can talk until we blue in the face it is no good

Felicia

Well keep your comments to yourself

Victor

Do you realize life and death is within each and every existing thing you do

Kay-Kay

You enduring tremendous sorrow for love please you know better Do you get smart when he going upside your head

Victor

Let me know what it is he doing so lovable is it that good I'm slacking if that is the case

Kay-Kay

Yeah we need to rebuild our love affair if that is the case you can't tell this girl nothing she hardheaded

Victor

Felicia when is enough enough when it is to late

Doctor

Most times it's enough when the children get hurt or die because of the abuse

Victor

(Looking around) Why do I see all these battered women no police

Kay-Kay

They hardheaded too No complaints, arrests, nothing

Felicia

Give it a rest will you two leave it alone

Doctor

That's why these women have been abused for so long they are scared

Kay-Kay

After you been hit so many times you think it's normal blind love

Victor

Why doesn't the state pick it up I couldn't even argue with my wife

Kay-Kay

Because ICU and Death are more important to these women

Felicia

I'm not pressing charges on Tucker my husband my problem

Doctor

Allow the most important factor in your life to be God as the center of your Will

Victor

You and my grand-babies stay well connected to God stay faithful Felicia

Kay-Kay

What you all nervous for this isn't your first time here

Victor

Your mother and I came to tell you goodbye this is it

Kay-Kay

We can't keep seeing you like it hurt too much when you wake up it is worthless to try and talk to you

Victor

Until things change you and my grand children are going to continue to suffer get it right

Doctor

> Hurting people hurt people that's all hurting people know how to do they know how to hurt you

Kay-Kay

> Sorrowful people don't start over to continue the suffering accept a change

2sweet

> (Excuse Me) Everybody it's my birthday Hey Hey!!

Kay-Kay/Victor

> Yelling 2sweet

2sweet

> And You Know This Momma You Know You Know This Man!!!

Felicia

> What are you doing you suppose to be in group see what I'm talking about

2sweet

> Hey Felicia, Grandma, Grandpa I couldn't let yall leave on my Birthday

Victor

> You will never heal if the wounds stay open hear me Felicia

2sweet

> Go Go Go shorty it's my birthday (17)

Kay-Kay

> We got to go until you make up your mind you sick and tired we can pray for you

Victor

> We can't help you this way we got to step back and pray without ceasing God is able

2sweet

Man I promise (Doctor-Family) If I see Tucker put his hands on momma one more time Ohh!!

Kay-Kay

2sweet calm down stay in a childs place now where you trying to run off too

Felicia

Some old Leadership program that's all he been talking about lately

Victor

Yeah, Learning about the Local Government I'm proud of my Boy here 2sweet take this money and don't spend in one day

2sweet

Peace God Bless you later a Thousand! Oops I'm loud! Thank You Jesus (Jumping around) counting money

Victor

That should take care of you now gone

Felicia

Buy Baby see you later peace Love you

Narrator

When you do wrong wrong follows you

Narrator

The Feds are already at C-Luv's House waiting on him to walk through the door

Narrator

C-Luv is headed to the spot whistling carrying a Duffle Bag full of illegal substances

Narrator

As C-Luv enters the spot the Feds chase him out the house he's yelling

Narrator

Det. Reggie is on the chase yelling for C-Luv to stop stop right there

Narrator

C-Luv Yelling at the Feds put your guns down put your guns down

Det. Reggie

Still Pointing his gun chasing C-Luv

Det Trent

C-Luv please don't make this situation worse than it has to be for yourself

C-Luv

The last person held at gun point by the police in this neighborhood was shot dead in cold blood you really want to talk

Det Reggie

You don't even know what we want your just acting guilty for no reason

C-Luv

I must fit the description why you chasing me. This occasion can't be good it just can't be good

Det. Reggie

Seriously man what you doing on this side of town anyway we banded you from this side months ago

C-Luv

> Why should I trust that you will put your guns down put your guns down I can't concentrate staring at the gun barrels.

Det. Reggie

> What you talking about C-Luv we need some good information stop playing around

C-Luv

> What police Academy did you graduate from Wal-Mart parking lot security

Det. Trent

> You always got to be a comedian a sign of weakness partner just like your parents

C-Luv

> You mena to tell me yall went through all this chasing and raiding me to ask me why I'm over here the world is coming to an end for sure Help us Jesus

Det. Reggie

> You know the Deal C-Luv you know the deal you're parents told us to come and get you

Det. Trent

> Your mom and dad want to talk to you before they leave

Narrator

> C-Luv punches his hands yelling to himself The Deal I knew something was going wrong

C-Luv

> Straight up The deal you serious I knew it I'm putting my gun down don't try to get a promotion all you flashlight cops

Det. Reggie

> They said the deal hurry up when you visit with your parents you will only have (15-min)

C-Luv

> I knew it I'm putting my gun down don't try to get a raise by hurting me

Det. Trent

> If you don't try nothing we will not try anything

C-Luv

> Hey alright now I'm telling you I shoot back you better be glad they said the deal

Det. Reggie

> C-Luv do you realize that scared people with guns kill people not law abiding citizens

C-Luv

> Welcome to the jungle and for future reference don't pull guns on people unless you all should know the saying better than me

Det. Trent

> Yeah Yeah Unless we want one pulled on us

C-Luv

> I know they taught you that in the academy I know it they taught you that in the Academy

Det. Trent

> Yeah, Yeah since you know it why make matters worse

C-Luv

> So why on earth would you yell me to put my gun down when you got one pulled on me already

Det. Reggie

It's Different we know who you are C-Luv when people know who you are especially police it makes it easier to deal with you

C-Luv

Yall tripping put you gun down freeze what's all that please in my projects Crooks dress up like the police it's ashame huh but they do it

C-Luv

Matter of fact where were yall at the other night when ray got shot twice in the back we called 911 at ten o clock. The police came the next day cowards

The Conversation with Jeena-Sylvester ©

Narrator

Sylvester/Jeena

They are in the holding Tank in County Jail

Jeena

Vester You know how C-Luv is we got to tell him the truth we got to tell him something

Sylvester

I don't aim to lie to the boy never have never will yeah we gone tell him how we got in this mess

Det. Leslie

Whatever you say to him you better make it quick (15-min) isn't that long

Jeena

I refuse to rot in prison wondering did I tell him the entire story

Sylvester

> If C-Luv rejects us as being good parents forgive him it was bound to happen we were not great examples

Jeena

> C-Luv got to hear the truth no matter how terrible we feel we got to inspire him to do the right thing in life he still got a chance

Sylvester

> Remember C-Luv isn't thinking about right or wrong he thinking about selling drugs

Jeena

> We raised him to have choices right I know we did we tried to do the best we could

Sylvester

> C-Luv cares about bright clothes and Jordans that's all right now we showed him the materialistic side of life

Jeena

> Sure got that right I don't know why that boy buys those shoes that he only wears one time

Jeena

> He Only Wear them One Time just spoiled

Sylvester

> He Only Wear One Time that isn't spoiled that's arrogant

Det. Leslie

> I never understood that either why do they waste their money

Jeena

What we gone do when he get here

Sylvester

Walking around everybody want to be a thug wanting things for free

Jeena

Everybody want to go to heaven don't nobody want to suffer

Sylvester

Sorry everyone will not be going to heaven

Det. Leslie

You can't count all people out or condemn we are all God's Children

Sylvester

But, But

Jeena

But when did you start studdering today

Sylvester

We have not done anything but what we were allowed to do see where all that tough stuff got us

Jeena

Don't sell another line of that non-sense you keep this true do you hear me we owe C-Luv that much respect to be honest

Sylvester

You can make more money in Hollywood acting like a thug these days and C-Luv will not listen to us

Jeena

This is real life reality real people real facts of life problems he don't have no choice but to listen

Sylvester

> C-Luv does know right from wrong life is about choices

Jeena

> I'm telling my son the truth things got out of control we were in it for the money things got out of control

Sylvester

> There is only one way to live right God's Way the right way

Jeena

> We didn't have control we lost it we became powerless to the game

Det. Leslie

> You can't mix right and wrong and figure nothing out did you go to church

Jeena

> All the greed, lust, and envy got in the way when the killing started

Sylvester

> We chose the wrong path after that the deceitful lifestyle ruined us

Jeena

> Life is not a cartoon it is real everything about it is real you can't cover up a lie the truth will prevail

Sylvester

We took care of C-Luv we went over board to protect
him

Jeena

The future is in God's hands may C-Luv find help
through Jesus our Lord and saviour

Sylvester

All the children's Future is in God's hands C-Luv isn't
the only one out there in harms way

Jeena

You are right Help the children Jesus Help Them

Sylvester

We can't help him now we got enough problems
this is a personal relationship with Jesus

Jeena

C-Luv can't say we didn't try to take care of him the
right way

Det. Leslie

Parents tend to battle with their own problems
missing the whole point

Sylvester

We battled with our own mess so long we let C-Luv
get out of control you are so true

Jeena

We chose this road don't be like us this is the end
result

Sylvester

If you make choices like us this is what you will have
to face or worse the thug life will land you in jail
prison and the early grave

Jeena

> Consequences that come along with bad decisions are prison and death

Sylvester

> You always got a choice just decide how you want to live good or bad either way we all got a grave to look forward to

Det. Leslie

> It is all up to you as an individual to lead a productive life

Sylvester

> C-Luv   Before you hit those streets again ask yourself how you gone live

Jeena

> YOU GONE LIVE WITH GOD-
> GOD'S WILL OR WITHOUT GOD

Sylvester

> YOU GONE LIVE WITH GOD-
> GOD'S WILL OR WITHOUT GOD

Det. Leslie

> For two knuckleheads C-Luv they truly love you man

C-Luv

> Love Love Man How you know they love me

Det. Trent

> 1st of all it was your parents idea to visit with you I could careless

Narrator

> Det. Reggie Hands C-luv a card

C-Luv

Why do yall keep handing me cards you think I'm a snitch too

DET. ALL

We are all just doing our jobs no more or less we want to help you

C-Luv

All they ever showed me was street love-Thug Love

Det. Reggie

They could have let you see this on the news or in the newspaper they chose to visit with you face to face have more compassion for your parents

C-Luv

Yeah I could have been looking bogus in the projects for a while running for my life cause people think I am a snitch too

Det. Reggie

Show some respect for your parents who you gone live for now C-Luv you know right from wrong

C-Luv

All I ever heard was C-Luv cook this, bag that, dope in my pampers

Det. Leslie

It is not worth it in the end for you to blame yourself

C-Luv

The streets need love hear me out for 10 years that's all I heard huh Vester!!

Det. Leslie

Don't be the reason you fail

C-Luv

Sylvester use to say we hustle because people can't afford Medicaid or medicare

Det Reggie

Treat yourself right all you got is you God is in control now if you let him

C-Luv

I'm Mr. Pharmacy to these streets keeping the thugs employed

Sylvester

You making a huge mistake C-Luv you are making a huge mistake

C-Luv

You told me I was supposed to been aborted when I was conceived a complete mess up

Det. Trent

You got three minutes

C-Luv

I would have ruined your life you two disgrace me and I can't be upset

Det. Reggie

Calm down C-Luv it's alright just Calm Down

C-Luv

Cowards all about yourselves Ahh Mr. Officer Det. Leslie

Det. Leslie

Yeah, C-Luv what is it

C-Luv

Do you have children if so how many and speak up I can't hear you

Det. Leslie

Yes two girl and boy

C-Luv

When did you know your lifestyle had to change
speak up

Det. Leslie

When my wife told me (instantly) it's not like that
for everyone

C-Luv

Sylvester you hear that a proud dad responsible look
at you now (Mark)

Chauncey

Come on C-Luv times up take it easy

C-Luv

I pray you two knuckleheads don't drop the soap

Narrator

C-Luv LEAVING THE COUNTY JAIL

Narrator

C-Luv rapping IS THIS IT
THIS HOW YALL GONE DO ME
LIFE AND DEATH IS WITHIN:
Each STEP, BLINK, INHALE, EXHALE,
THOUGHT, GESTURE, AND ACT

Narrator

C-LUV
I'M LIVING TO DIE AND HELL CAN'T HOLD ME
C-LUV
OH YEAH JEENA-SYLVESTER DON'T CALL ME I WILL
CALL YOU
HA HA HA

(C-Luv)

(Headed to leadership program)

Narrator

Reporter's Harass-

C-Luv On the way into visit Jeena-Sylvester

Narrator

C-Luv On his way into the County-Jail

Narrator

Reporter's

They are asking several questions

News

The Newspaper is on location outside jail

Reporter's

Today the F.B.I seal deal on Informer's Jeena-Sylvester

Reporter's

Authorities say this is a Big Problem in the Bureau for Undercover agents

C-Luv

Continues to walk on ignoring the questions and comments

Reporter's

The Informers became King-Pins of Cartels and Detectives retire crooked

C-Luv

The war on drugs and crime has been since the beginning of time

Reporter's

The Luv Family is known as the Hub for the illegal activity

C-Luv

Our Moto is everything is for sale we are like Super Wal-Mart we got it for cheap

Reporter's

Prime example of a corrupt system we finally got the Luv family

C-Luv

You want cheap health care coverage ball out of control Ha Ha we the best

Reporter's

The Indictments are coming to a 30 year end of corruption

Reporter's

C-Luv would you like to comment on any of these allegations

C-Luv

You already stated your facts we got 3 for $50 and 7 for a $100 since the 70's

Narrator

(Idol Time) is the Devils workshop

Narrator

Man-Man/Duke/C-Luv
They are already at Leadership Program waiting to get into something

Narrator

Tucker Suppose to be on the way to the hospital for
Extended Family Group Counseling
With his family

Narrator

As Tucker approaches the leadership program area

Narrator

Man-Man yelling at Tucker Hey
Wuz up ol'skool you doing good I see

Tucker

Grinning wildly Huh Huh

Narrator

Duke (Gestures) like he is hardcore

Duke

Where my money at

Narrator

C-Luv
Just throws up the deuces
C-Luv
I don't want no part in nothing you got going on

Tucker

Yall want to make a couple stacks I'm in a hurry well
do yall

Man-Man

Right on what's really good you always up to no-good
tucker we need our money now

Duke

Spit it out ol'skool what's up pay us up front or do it
yourself

Tucker

I want 2sweet killed and you can run the eastside

C-Luv

Count me out fight your own Battles don't you got enough drama in your life I know I do

Man-Man

You can get it to C-luv we no 2sweet your homeboy

Duke

Scared money don't make no money

C-Luv

Tucker you just an old Domestic Violence King and Man-man and Duke are your Two Stoogers I have saw it all now

Tucker

Handle it ASAP hear me handle it

Narrator

Tucker counting out money to Man-Man/Duke

Man-Man

C-Luv you got a problem I can see that it is bothering you get it off your chest right now player

C-Luv

I got workers working for me with better things to do then get in trouble dealing with yall busters get a life

Man-Man

Long as you know the code on the streets snitches get stitches

Duke

Remember that C-Luv remember it

Tucker

>I'll holla at yall later peace

C-Luv

>You are out of your ever loving mind if you think I'm conspiring to murder my only homeboy. The two idiots in the hood please

Man-Man

>Stand in our way you will get it too C-Luv

Duke

>I told you before stop playing C-Luv if you scared go to church

C-Luv

>You are both smoking what you been selling I go to church for blessing and healing for instruction not because I'm scared busters think that way yall got what's coming to you Believe that

Narrator notes:

(Tucker)

>-gone to Family Counseling to pick-up his family for church

(C-Luv)

>-At Leadership Program getting ready to rap his song

(Man-Man/Duke)

>-At Program plotting to fight with 2sweet

Counselor

> Excuse me settle down you are here to get better relax feel free to express yourself

Pristine

> Honestly, I think someone should put Tucker in prison I know he's my dad but that's how I feel I mean it soon as we leave this meeting

Counselor

> Excuse me we will have order in these sessions I know that you all have attitudes but we must maintain order starting out by stating your name before you speak

Jax

> I am Jax and we need to calm down. This place feels better already after all we have been through settle down

Counselor

> I'm here to help you find a solution to the problem no cure I don't have all the answers we have to work together all of us have a story

Narrator
Tucker

> Sitting back smiling playing with his cell phone Ha Ha Ha!!!

Jax

> If this is better than the grave the grave must be heaven to the victims in this place

Counselor

> You are all full of bitterness which is quite normal at this stage of development why are you here can anyone tell me that

Pristine

> We are here to try and get better by creating some useful tactics in our mentality when faced with problems our problem is dealing with people who promise only to make themselves look good

Counselor

> Tucker do you care to elaborate on these expressions from your children they really need your consideration

Jax

> Tucker don't care about this session everything is a joke one thing is for sure God is accusing the evil and the good right now Tucker

Pristine

> You're my dad I have to respect you nothing is over with Tucker you are the drama king

Jax

> God is accusing us as though he can't help himself it's not our fault we have parents who can't settle their differences like grown-ups it's not our fault

2sweet

> Hey Hey! Preach about that at church tonight Tucker we have suffered under your leadership for so long we sound like you when we are hurting it's not our fault we are here

Pristine

Fake preacher no members Tucker, You are a hypocrite Fake Fake as a four dollar bill fake God will not take second to this situation

Jax

Simply put Just stop putting your hands on our Mom and we will be okay

2sweet

Jesus refuses to share his bride Thank You Jesus Christ like isn't putting your hands on other people to feel good

Counselor

2sweet you are either leaving or take a seat and stay a while have a seat I know you're are angry that's what we are here for positive suggestions

Pristine

Everybody has their day good and bad your day is here but more so God's Judgment is upon the land

Tucker

I guess warning comes before destruction heard that before

2sweet

You sending threats now Tucker HUH! You got the nerve to sit there and threaten people you really don't care

Jax

We didn't hurt you so stop preaching that non-sense to us

Tucker

Have you ever fought with God about issues in life what issues did you fight with him about

2sweet

Catastrophies through God's eyes are endless cycles of war and death so regardless of your offense God is able to do exactly what he says vengeance is the Lords

Pristine

Tucker who do you think you are God You better stop playing with God

Jax

You will learn God meant for his people to have one love

Pristine

Yeah one true love God himself

2sweet

Remember that Tucker hahaha One Love-One Love-One Love

LEADERSHIP PROGRAM STARTS HERE

    C-Luv (2verses)

    2Sweets (2verses)

    Child Abuse Program

    Sylvester/Jeena Announce awareness

    Music and More

Slide 1

Child Abuse Prevention
Out–reach to overcome

A Leadership program in Act–1   C–Luv's Parents (Send a Surgeon Warning)

C–Luv Performs (Still–Suffering)
2Sweet Performs (I'm Up)
LOVE TEMPLE C.O.G.I.C. Performs The Theme Song
(Turn Your Life Around)
MCCEE TEMPLE C.O.G.I.C. Performs
1) Best of My Praise
2) Jesus Live
Eld. Scott–Message

Willie Pringle
Writer–Director

Slide 2

"Defend the cause of the weak and fatherless; maintain the rights of
the poor and oppressed. Rescue the weak and needy; deliver them
from the hand of the wicked." (Psalms 82:3–4)

Slide 3

Children under 1yr old account for
41% of all abuse related deaths
reported in 2002. Of those 76%
were younger than 4 years–old

Slide 4

A child abuse case is reported every 10 seconds.
~www.childhelp.org~

Slide 5

▸ "Child abuse casts a shadow the
length of a lifetime."
▸ –Herbert Ward

Slide 6

If you suspect child abuse

STOP–What you doing

QUIT–Thinking about yourself

NO–group of children are immune
to abuse

DON'T–Hesitate to be the voice
for the victims cry for help

TURN YOUR LIFE AROUND

(Verse-1)
THE COLDER IT GETS THESE DAYS
A CHANGE GOT TO BE MADE
THERE'S TO MUCH CRIME/ DECAY
POVERTY PEOPLE WE NEED TO PRAY
NO MORE STREET WARS/RAIDS,
HOMELESSNESS, CHILD ABUSE,
DOMESTIC VIOLENCE
WE NEED TO BE SINGING PSALMS
 FOR SOME PREACHERS
PREACHING TEACHING HOLINESS
GUIDING OUR WISHES AND RICHES
WE POVERTY STRICKEN BROKE
BUSTED AND DISGUSTED AND CAN'T
BE TRUSTED WITHOUT JESUS LOST
FEELING AS IF LIFE'S A BIG JOKE
ANOTHER HUSTLE GAMBLE
MONEY THE ROOT OF SINS BURNING
MY MIND LIKE CANDLES DIRTY
    WORKS
OF THE DEVIL FILLING US WITH NO
    HOPE
THE DEVIL IS A LIAR CHECK
    YOURSELF
CHECK YOUR SYMPATHY FOR
    CENTURIES
DEVILS BEEN ON THIS PATH JESUS
    THANKS
FOR YOUR EMPATHY WE CAN LOOK
    FOR A GREATER WRATH
THAT'S WHY I WROTE THIS
    TELEGRAPH
CLAIMING ETERNAL LIFE BY FAITH
HAVING HOPE FOR UNSEEN
    BLESSINGS
DREAMING OF THE POWER OF OUR
    FATHER
THE AUTHOR AND FINISHER
    CREATOR ALPHA OMEGA
    REDEEMER
THANK GOD FOR OUR LORD AND
    SAVOIR

HOLDING THE WHOLE WORLD IN HIS
    HANDS
HE'S MORE THAN THE WORLD
    AGAINST US
SATAN THE LORD REBUKE YOU
IN JESUS NAME THAT'S POWER
YOU CAN'T HOLD THE HOLY GHOST
NO CONTROL JUST SPIT VENOM
YOU CAN'T TAUNT ME
I'M TAKING HEED TEACHING
OUR SEEDS TO PRAY FOR THE
    TRINITY
MURDERERS DRUG DEALERS
    THEIVES
HAVE KILLED POLLUTED ROBBED
OUR WORLD PUSHING DOPE SEX
    AND MONEY
KEEPING US BROKE AND HUNGRY
SPIRITUALLY DEAD FIENDING LIKE
    WILD BEAST
THROUGH THESE STREETS FOR A
    CHANGE
IN JESUS NAME

(VERSE-2)
POLITICIANS SAY WE INCORRECT
WE ACT LIKE WE ONLY WANT
    HANDOUTS
WE DEAL WITH LESS STRESSED
    JOBLESS
GROWING UP IN ONE PARENT
    HOMES
FILLED WITH ABUSE AND RUNAWAYS
WHAT'S THAT TELLING US
CHILDREN PARENTLESS LEARNING
    LESS
NEIGHBORHOOD'S FULL OF LOW
    GROWTH
PEOPLE AT THE END OF THEIR ROPES
LOW DEVELOPED HOMES NO TRUST
THE CRIME RATES KEEPING US
    LOCKED UP
TRAGEDIES HAPPEN PEOPLE
    DEPRESSED

FAILING TO ADAPT TO PREJUDICE
EXISTING
PEOPLE IN PRISON WITH LOST SOULS
FEELING THE PAIN AND NO GOALS
FULL OF LOW FELONIOUS MORAL'S
CHILDREN LEARNING FELONIOUS
TEMPTATIONS
PRAYING FOR SUCCESS THROUGH
TESTS
CONQUERING OVERCOMING THE
WORLD
SEPERATING OURSELVES FROM
DRUGS
VIOLENCE SEX AND HELL
WE LIVING TO DIE AND FOREVER
LIVE
NO VICTIM OF CIRCUMSTANCES
WE TRYING TO TURN OUR LIFE
AROUND
TO LIVE AGAIN WITH JESUS

DEAR GOD, THE FATHER OF MY
LORD AND SAVOIR JESUS LOOK
DEEP INSIDE MY HEART AND
FIND MY NEED MY PARENTS
DID THEIR BEST I WAS ALWAYS
MISUNDERSTOOD I AM SAFE
WITH JESUS FORGIVE ME FOR MY
SINS
JESUS C-LUV IN PAIN YOU NO MY
SUFFERING JESUS C-LUV IN PAIN
YOU NO MY STRUGGLES STILL
SUFFERING
JESUS HAVE MERCY ON ME
MY PARENTS SHOWED ME STREET
LOVE
EVERYBODY PRAYING AINT MAKING
IT TO HEAVEN
PLEASE DELIVER ME FROM MY
DECEITFUL MENTALITY
JESUS I DON'T WANT TO BURN FOR
LEARNING
HOW TO COUNT GRAMS TO OUNCES

MY PARENTS COULD'VE TAUGHT ME
BETTER
INSTEAD IT WAS STREET LIFE
MAKING STINGS
WITH OUNCES OF DOPE ON ME
I'M SUPPLY AND DEMAND A
PHARMACIST
THEY CALL ME MR. ECONOMY ON
THE STREET
JESUS I DON'T WANT TO BURN
NO-NO
JESUS THIS PRAYERS TO YOU
I SURRENDER MY WILL MY HEART IS
HURTING
I DON'T KNOW WHAT TO DO I'M
CALLING
ON YOU I'M TRYING TO LIVE RIGHT I
WANNA QUIT
MY MEMORIES FADED AND SHADY
MY PARENTS RAISED ME CRAZY
JESUS KEPT ME ALIVE FOR A REASON
THAT'S WHY I'M PRAYING NOW
I'M STILL SUFFERING A SURVIVOR
SURVIVED BRUSHES WITH DEATH
STILL ALIVE TO TELL THIS STORY
TODAY I LIVE LIFE ON GOD'S TERMS
LIFE AND DEATH ARE IN THE
TONGUE
IN EVERY BREATH STEP MINUTE
BLINK
IT'S THERE YOU HAVE A CHOICE
JESUS
YOU ARE MY ALPHA OMEGA GUILTY
TIL YOU JUDGE ME
I ADMIT I'M GUILTY I DON'T WANT
TO BURN
JESUS THAT'S UNWORTHY FORGIVE
ME
I WAS A WILD AS A JUVENILE
RAN WITH GANGS IN THE MEAN
WHILE
I NO RIGHT FROM WRONG
I LOVE STREET LIFE BALLING TIL I
FALL OFF

YEAH I LOVE CHURCH TO I DON'T
WANT TO GO TO HELL
RAISED IN THE DOPE GAME
I THOUGHT I COULDN'T BE FAITHFUL
JESUS I'M SO MISERABLE THE
STREETS
WERE MY ESCAPE GOAT HOW CAN
I REPAY
YOU JESUS YOU KEEP ME ALIVE EVEN
WHEN I DON'T DESERVE IT
YOU SHINE THROUGH IT ALL
CONSISTENTLY!

(VERSE-2)
JESUS THANK YOU FOR TURNING ME
INTO A MAN
WATCHING OVER MY PARENTS IN
PRISON
YOU SAW HOW WE ERE LIVING
I GOTTA CHANGE THE DEVIL TRYING
TO KILL US
KEEP US SAFE MY PARENTS WON'T
BE AROUND
TO PROMOTE MY HUSTLES I NEED
YOU
I NEED YOUR GUIDANCE
JESUS I'LL TELL YOU WHEN I'M
SCARED
WHEN NOBODIES PREACHING THE
GOSPEL
KEEP MY ENEMIES FROM CAUSING
HARM
MY PARENTS SNITCHING I'M TRUE
TO THE GAME
NO SNITCH IN ME THANKS FOR ALL
YOUR BLESSINGS
ALLOWING ME THE STRENGTH TO
FIGHT OFF THE WORLD
I AINT NO KILLA BUT DON'T PUCH
ME
JESUS IF THEY THINK I'M A SNITCH
I'M A SINNER'S SON BORN TO A
SINNERS WORLD

SAVED BY GRACE HEART TURNED
INTO A HEART OF FLESH
TRANSFORMED
OUT OF SIN AND SHAME BY GOD
NOT MY MOM OR POP IN GOD'S
WILL
I AINT INFORMING NOTHING BUT
TRUTH
THEY TRIED TO RUIN ME THROUGH
THAT
WITCH AND WARLOCK SPIRIT
JESUS WAS RIGHT THERE SAYING
PRAY
I WILL BE RIGHT THERE PRAYING
DENYING FLESH AND PRIDE
GETTING ALL THE TEARS OUT THAT I
HELD INSIDE
VENGENCE IS THE LORDS HE REPLY'S
IF SOMEONE TRIES TO HARM ME I'LL
BE WRITING ANOTHER PRAYER
ASKING GOD TO PLEASE HELP ME
AMEN!

(VERSE-1)
IT'S A MUST THAT I'M UP
I LIVED HELL ON EARTH
DYING DAILY LOOKING FOR HEAVEN
REPENTING KEEPNG A STEADY FLOW
SEEKING FOR PEACE THE LIVING
GOD
TAKING IT SLOW AS TIME PASS
MOVING UP AND MOVING ON
RAISING THE PRAISIES UP
PRAYERS MOVE MOUNTAINS
WHEN TIMES GET HARD PRAY TO
GOD
THEN PRAY EVEN HARDER DON'T
STRESS
STRESS WILL EXPLODE YOUR HEART
I DON'T WANT TO GO BACK
MY DAUGHTER'S NEED A MEAL
BEAN'S RICE CORN BREAD OR
CEREAL
GIVING LIVING ALL I GOT
AVOIDING THE SCAMS AND PLOTS

OFF GRRAMS AND ROCKS
IF A SITUATION PRESENTS ITSELF
I'M ON MY PRAYER CIRCLE
CALLING THE FATHER OF MY LORD
    AND SAVOIR
JESUS THE SON OF MAN SET ME
    FREE
POWERED BY THE HOLY GHOST
    FASTING
COVERED IN THE BLOOD OF JESUS
REMEMBER THE WORD NEVER FAILS
IT'S STRONGER THAN TIMBER
COLDER THAN THE COLDEST STREETS
    IN MICHIGAN IN THE WINTER

(CHORUS)
IT'S A MUST THAT I'M UP
AFTER DUCK TIL DAWN
PRAYING TO MY FATHER IN HEAVEN
FOR STRENGTH TO FAST AND CARRY
    THE MESSAGE ON AND ON
IN THE NAME OF JESUS!
JESUS SAVED A SINNER I SURRENDER
    TO THE WILL OF GOD
I HAD TO CHANGE PEOPLE PLACES
    THINGS ADMITTING
I'M NOT PERFECT BORN AGAIN INTO
    A RIGHTEOUS ROUTE
ACCEPTING JESUS AS MY LORD AND
    SAVOIR STRENGTHENS ME
ACEPTANCE IS THE KEY FOR ME TO
    BATTLE AGAINST DECEIT
THE WORLD REMAINS THE SAME I
    MUST CHANGE PRINCIPALITIES
ASKING GOD FOR GUIDANCE
    SEEKING FOR PEACE FORGIVE ME
JESUS IS KNOCKING ON MY DOOR
I GOT TO LET HIM IN I CHOOSE TO
    FOLLOE JESUS
INTO THE KINDOM I CAME TO
    BELIEVE IN
ONLY JESUS CAN SET ME FREE FROM
    POWERLESSNESS
AND UNMANAGEABLE ALCOHOL
    CONTROLLED ME

I RAN TO THE IN-CROWD INSTEAD
    OF GOD
GOD HEALED MY SCHIZOPHRENIA
    TOOK MY DESIRE FOR ALCOHOL
WIPED AWAY MY PAIN RESTORED
    PRESSURE WITH PEACE
THE HUMILITAION WAS PUSHED OUT
    REPLACED WITH HUMILITY
GOD NEVER LEFT I LEFT GOD I PRAY I
    NEVER LEAVE AGAIN
JESUS FILL ME WITH THE HOLY
    GHOST THE WORLDS OUT OF
    CONTROL
PREPARE ME FOR YOUR RETURN I
    WANT TO BE READY
READY FOR A ROOM IN YOUR
    FATHERS MANSION
RIDING ON GOLD PAVED ROADS
I GREW UP DISOBEDIENT
    WITNESSING YOUR MINISTRY
IT'S NOT ABOUT POPULARITY
JESUS YOU GOT MY MIND BODY AND
    SOUL YOU ARE IN CONTROL
I'M FEELING REFRESHED WRITINGS A
    BLESSING
I'M ONE OF THE BEST SCRIBES
    VERSUS HARDER THEN 40 YEARS
    OF ISOLATION
BAD I'M SAVED THE DEVILS MAD
    WITH MORE WONDERS
THEN A WALKING NOMAD TAKING
    THE MESSAGE

FROM PLACE TO PLACE
SEND IT BRING IT HOWEVER GOD
    USES ME
THROUGH CHRIST I CAN DO ALL
    THINGS
JESUS GIVES ME THE STRENGTH TO
    HAVE THE ABILITY
AND OPPORTUNITY TO BE A
    GRATEFUL WITNESS OF HIS LOVE
    FOR ALL HUMANITY

SYLVESTER/JEENA'S ANNOUNCEMENT
AFTER SENTENCE TO C-LUV!!!

THIS IS A TEST OF THE NATIONAL BROADCAST
SYSTEMS
ALERT ALERT BEWARE BEWARE
YOU NEED TO EVACUATE YOUR SPOTS CHANGE YOUR
HUSTLES TURN YOUR LIFE AROUND
THE DARKSIDE OF STREET LIFE WILL KILL YOU
C-LUV IF YOU'RE LISTENING TO THIS
THE SURGEON GENERAL WARNS WEL SO CAN WE!!!
DRUGS/ALCOHOL ROBS YOU OF YOUR R.I.G.H.T.S!!

R-RESPONSIBILITY
I-INTEGRITY
G-GOALS
H-HUMILITY
T-TRUST
S-SELF-RESPECT

WE NEED TO BREAK THE CHANGE OF WHERE WE COME FROM REGARDLESS OF WHERE OUR LIVES HAVE DRIVEN US WE CAN DO THE NEXT RIGHT THING YOU GOT PLENTY OF CHOICES LISTEN UP YOU ALWAYS HAVE A CHOICE THE RIGHT CHOICES OR THE WRONG CHOICES YOU CAN'T MIX THE TWO AND PLAY EITHER OR LOOK AT US WE ARE EXAMPLES OF WHAT NOT TO DO DON'T LET THIS BECOME YOUR WAY OF LIFE

THIS HAS BEEN A NATIONAL WHERE WE COME FROM SURGEON GENERAL WARNING

STOP ROBBING YOURSELF OF THE HONEST LUXURIES OF LIFE AND PEACE

TRUE STORY

HIGH SCHOOL PARENTING
MAKING WEDDING PLAN'S
HEADED TO THE ARMY
TRYING TO BECOME A MAN
2 BE ALL THAT I CAN
ALCOHOLIC WEED ABUSING MAN
IN BASIC TRAINING
THOUGHT I'D BE HAPPY
HAPPINESS WAS MY PLAN
USED TO RUN THE STREETS
GETTING SHOT AT PLAYING
PETTY HUSTLING TO STAY HYPE
DRUNK AND PARTY ALL NIGHT
BACKS AGAINST THE WORLD
WED TO MY BABY MOTHER
CAUSE SHE HAD MY BABY GIRL
LOOKING FOR OTHER GIRLS
MACKING AND CHEATING ON HER
USED TO LIVING ALCOHOLIC
BORN IN SIN NO LIE
NO WONDER I WAS LIVING TO DIE
MY STOMACH PAINS BAD APPENDIX
THAT'S HOW REAL THE LUST WAS
LIKE THE KLUMPS AT THE BUFFET
THEY FED THEIR APPETITE
I GOT TO ADMIT IN MANY WAYS
TEMPTED BY A LOT OF MISTRESSES

THEY NEVER TOUCHED MY HEART

I NEVER GAVE THEM MY BEST

JUST THE BOTTOM OF MY BUSINESS

I GOT A LOT OF LOVE FOR LADIES

I COULDN'T THEM THE TRUTH

SHOULD'VE TOLD THEM

STEP OFF GET LOST

THIS IS TO MUCH DISRESPECT

I CAN'T HAVE AN AFFAIR

ON MY BABY MOM

SHE'S AT HOME

ABOUT TO HAVE MY CHILD

I CAN'T HAVE THEM ALL

I KNOW I WAS DOING WRONG

GOT OFFERES TO EAT OUT

LEAVING MY DINNER AT HOME

THE OLD WILLIE WASN'T PRAYING

OR GOD FEARING

I HAD TO MUCH LOVE FOR LADIES

God,

   The Father, of my Lord, and Savior, Jesus Christ. Who is the head of my life. Today, Father you are my light in my darkest moments, my salvation I shall fear no man. I got the fear of God in me as the Holy Ghost. Forgive me Father for I have sinned and fallen short against you this is thirty four years in the making. I didn't know that I had the ability to forgive myself I was innocent. God is the strength of my life I shall not be afraid. Today I am still suffering but not as harsh as It were before I turned my will to your will. I am learning form my mistakes as truth comes to pass I'm a grateful recovering Alcoholic.

(Verse-1)

I WENT THRU HELL TO GET HERE
39 MOS AND 26 DAYS IN THE MAKING
THE CREATION OF GOD
NO SIDE DEALS WITH ENEMIES
GOD THE FATHER BEEN
DEALING WITH ME HOLY GHOST
USED TO ASK PEOPLE
WHAT'S PRAYER PRAYER'S
KEPT ME FOCUSED ON GOD
FOCUSED ON ME AND RECOVERY
PRAYERS SAVED ME FROM ALCOHOL
I SHOULD'VE DIED OUT THERE
I LOVED ALCOHOL MORE
WHEN IT TRIED TO KILL ME
A BINGE DEAD BEAT DAD PROUD
FALSE FANTASY LIVING FOR 13
CHILDREN 16-14 CALL ME DAILY
MY OLDEST LIVES WITH ME
PRAYERS HELP ME STAY SAVE
PRAYERS KEPT ME ALIVE IN 95
WHEN THEM BULLETS CUT THE AIR
I BEEN SHOT AT NEVER SHOT
I SHOULD'VE FELL THEN PRAYING
PRAYERS MEDICINE TO THE SPIRIT
HEALING WOUNDS IN/EXTERNALLY
ASK THE PEOPLE STILL SUFFERING
I WAS SPIRITUALLY DEAD

A CO-DEPENDENT TO MISERY
LIVING ISOLATED AS DEAD PEOPLE
THE IN-CROWD KEPT ME GOING
SURRENDERING HELPED ME REALIZE
POWER IN PRAYERS

(CHORUS)
ALL I HAD TO DO WAS GET ON MY KNEES
CLOSE MY EYES PUT MY HANDS TOGETHER
BOW MY HEAD ASK GOD TO KEEP ME
ON THE RIGHT PATH OUT OF JAILS
INSTITUTIONS BEFORE THE NEXT STEP
BE DEATH PLEASE PROTECT CHILDREN
SAVE OUR FAMILIES DEAR GOD HERE I AM
I REPENT MY SINS FORGIVE ME
FOR MY MISTAKES THE PAIN RUNS DEEP
FORGIVE ALL THE DISRESPECTFUL NIGHTS
I MADE MOM CRY THE RUNNING WILD
IN THE STREETS GOD FORGIVE ME

(VERSE-2)
I PRAY TO GOD TO STRENGTHEN ME
I DID HARMFUL THINGS IN MY PAST
THY WILL BE DONE WIPE IT AWAY
THE OLD WAY WILL NEVER HAPPEN
PRAYER TAKES THE PAIN AWAY
USED TO COULDN'T SPEAK ON IT
GOD GIFTED MY WRITING SKILLS
USED TO CULDN'T SLEEP HOMIE

NOW STRENGTHEN MY WEAKNESSES

I CAN TAKE THE PAIN WITH THE LOSSES

PRAYING MORE CARRYING MY CROSS

LIVING ON BORROWED TIME FORGIVE ME

A SINNER SINNNING GOT ME WHERE I AM

PRAYING DAILY TO MAKE IT

PRAYING PRAYERS REGARDLESS

IF THE HURT IS THERE

I THANK GOD FOR SHOWING ME

HE TRULY CARES ABOUT ME

I WILL NOT SHUT DOWN

MY CAPABILITIES ARE IMMACULATE

BY THE GRACE AND MRECY OF GOD

I WILL MAN UP TO MY PROBLEMS

SENDING PRAYERS IN THE AIR

(VERSE-3)

I USED TO LIVE A WILD HOGS LIFE

WHERE I'M AT MY HOME

NOW I'M DOWN ON MY KNEES PRAYING

BLESSED MOANING AND GROANING

LIFE IS MUCH BETTER THE BEST

LIVING PEACEFULLY JOYOUS

THROUGH THE LONG SUFFERING

WHETHER WALKING OR RIDING A BIKE

RAIN SLEET OR SNOW STILL GRATEFUL

LIFE KEEPS MOVING ON AND ON

GOD IS ALWAYS THERE THICK OR THIN

I'M THINKING HOW MOM BATTLED

BETWEEN TWO ALCOHOLIC ADDICTIONS

HAROLD JAMES REST IN PEACE

PROVES MOM WAS JUST AS SICK

AS YOU AND ME GETTING BETTER

I GOT A THREE PAGE RESUME

LIVING A LIE I COULDN'T KEEP

A 9-5 WONDERING WHY

PARANOID ON THEM STREETS BOOZED UP

BEYOND BELIEF WAS HOMOCIDE

SCHIZOPHRENIC LIVING FOR THE IN-CROWD

SUICIDE IT TOOK 31 YEARS TO GET 39MOS

PLUS 26DAYS SOBER I SURRENDERED

MY WILL TO GOD'S WILL GOD SENT ME

TO ANOTHER WAY AGAIN LITERALLY

SO I COULD ADMIT IT

ACCEPT IT AND DECIDE TO QUIT IT

ASKING GOD TO BE MY LORD AND SAVIOR

IS THE WAY FOR ME BECAUSE

I JUST COULDN'T GET RIGHT

This is the realist I ever wrote the chorus is the same as Ke-Ke's but your verse is your verse!!!

(Chorus)

Daddy,

Why are you gone so long

Daddy,

When you gone come back home

Daddy,

You gotta get your drink and party on

Daddy,

When you gone come back home

(VERSE-1)

JASMINE I THINK ABOUT YOU ALL THE TIME

EVEN WHEN I USED TO NEGLECT YOU SIPPING WINE

I REMEMBER THE LONELY TIMES AND START CRYING

WHY DID I SUFFER THE MISERY PAIN AND SHAME

KNOWING HOW MY DAD LEFT ME

WHY DID I DO THE SAME

YOU WITH ME IN MY MORNING NOON AMD NIGHTLY PRAYERS

YOUR PART OF MY TEARS SHED FOR DAILY FEARS

YOU'RE MY LIFE STORY IN TESTIMONY I SHARE

I REMEMBER YOUR BIRTHDAYS WERE THE WORSE DAYS

I USED TO SIP BEER AND LIQUOR THIRSTY

YES I LOVE THE LIFE I LIVE

JASMINE I WENT FROM – TO +

AND IT'S ALL GOOD I SEE GOD'S PROMISE

SIGNS FOR THE FUTURE SO DIVINE

HOPE YOU AND YUR MOM DOING FINE

 I LOVE MYSELF I CAN LOVE YOU

I USED TO BE A DEAD BEAT DAD

MOST OF OUR LIFE TOGETHER

I'M STRAIT YOU CAN HUG DADDY TIGHT

WHEN I'M WITH YOU LONLINESS IS GONE

SEEING YOU TAKES OFF THE EXTRA LOAD

YOU ARE A NEW BRAND AT STAR BUCKS

SMOOTH DARK CHOCOLATE CARAMEL

THE BEST SMILE YOU ARE A BENTON HARBOR JEWEL

TAKE PRIDE IN BEING TEACHABLE BABY

LEADERS HAVE TO FOLLOW AND LISTEN

I'M GOING TO KEEP REDISCOVERING LIFE

LIVING RIGHT RECOVERING FROM ALCOHOL

IT'S WHAT GOT ME THIS CLOSE TO YOU

CLOSE YOUR EYES SURPRISE LET'S PRAY

GOD'S WILL GIVES US WHATEVER WE WANT

JUST ACCEPT BELIEVE AND DECIDE

DO THE RIGHT THING

ON TOP OF A BILLION POSITIVE MINUTES

DADDY CAN RIDE FOR YOU

UNTIL I AM OLD GRAY AND TIRED FOR YOU

SO WHEN I AM DEAD AN GONE

YOU WILL UNDERSTAND I TRIED FOR YOU

IT'S IMPORTANT FOR GIRLS TO KNOW THEIR FATHER

I'M GOING TO BE THE MAN YOU RUN TO WHEN TIMES GET HARDER

YOUR IN MY HEART THAT'S GOD'S HOME

GOD CREATED THAT PLACE FOR YOU

THIS YEAR IT'S FOR ME T SHOW YOU

ALL THE LOVE I HAVE FOR YOU

MY FOUNDATION FOR US TO LIVE 4LIFE

I'M GEARING UP IN AGE

GETTING AS OLD AS I FEEL

I WILL STILL BE THERE FOR YOU

REGARDLESS SO JUST CHILL

NOTHING BUT THE LOVE OF GOD

COMPARES TO THE LOVE I GOT FOR YOU

NOTHING NO ALCOHOL DRUGS WOMEN

NOTHING CAN COME CLOSE TO THIS LOVE

IT'S ALL YOURS LIKE IT OR NOT HEARD ME

JASMINE THAT'S A RAP MAY YOU HAVE THE STRENGTH TO REJOICE IN PEACE JOY AND LONG-SUFFERING FOREVER AMEN!!!

I LOVE YOU JASMINE THIS IS ALL I COULD AFFORD AT THE TIME OF THE FIRST WRITING OF THIS I PRAY THAT GOD MAY BLESS THIS TO PRODUCE TREMENDOUS GIFTS TO GIVE OTHERS AT CHRISTMAS TIME FOR YEARS TO COME MERRY CHRISTMAS AND HAPPY NEW YEAR'S LOVE YOUR DADDY WILLIE X. PRINGLE ORGINAL 13TH DEC 2008 AT 10:42PM IN MORGANFIELD, KY

THIS IS THE REALIST I EVER WROTE, KE-KE MERRY CHRISTMAS/ HAPPY NEW YEARS TO YOU!!!

(Chorus) Same

(Verse)

I WAS LIVING LIFE THRU BINGE DRINKING AND ANGER

YOU WERE 14 FOR 13 I WASN'T THERE FOR YOU

I ALWAYS HAD ANTOHER DRUNKEN EXCUSE

A DEAD BEAT DAD LIVING FALSE FANTASY

KEKE I DESERVE THE SORROW THAT CAME TO ME

ALL I WANTED WAS FOR YOU TO RUN TO ME

I MISS WHEN YOU WERE A BABY

REACHING OUT TO PICK YOU UP

MOST OF THE TIME I WAS TO DRUNK

IF I WOULD HAVE TRIED TO PICK YOU UP

WE WOULD HAVE FELL YOU NEVER WOULD FORGIVE ME

ALL THAT PRETENDING IS FOR HOLLYWOOD

ALL THOSE THUGS ARE DEAD OR IN JAIL

I CAN'T LIVE ANOTHER DAY IN THE LIFE OF A LIE

AINT ENOUGH INVENTIONS TO PROVE HOW MUCH YOU MEAN TO ME

YOU ARE M ORE PRECIOUS TEHN BUILDINGS FULL OF PRADA SUEDE

I WANT TO SEE YOU BLOW CANDLES OUT ON BIRTHDAY CAKE

I WANT TO BE IN YOUR LIFE WHEN YOU MAKE GOOD/BAD
MISTAKES

THERE'S ONLY SO MUCH YOUR MOM CAN DO FOR YOU

SHE DOES SO MUCH AND STAND FIRM FOR YOU

ONLY A DAD CAN PREPARE YOU FOR THE LINES AND LIES

THEM GUYS GONE TRY TO SELL TO YOU

YOUR MOM STRONG SHE FELL FOR LINES/LIES TO

YOU DON'T BELIEVE ME LOOK AT YOUR REFLECTION

THE TRUTH I'M HERE SOBER TOO

I'M LEARNING NOT TO BE FOOLISH

IF THIS WORLD WAS MINE

I WOULD MAKE ANOTHER ONE 4 YOU

KEKE YOU THE NEW MEANING OF CRAZY SEXY COOL

YOU GOT IT FROM YOUR HANDSOME DAD AND LOVELY MOM

MERRY CHRISTMAS/HAPPY NEW YEARS

I LOVE YOU BABY GIRL PEACE JOY AND REJOICE IN LONG SUFFERING
ALWAYS HOLLA AT ME!!!

First giving Honor to God the Father of my Lord and Savior Jesus Christ for making all of this possible. I would like to Honor every last person in the building today we are all equally important in God's eyes. I know many of you are very familiar with the story of Christ Jesus. Prepare for one of the best summaries of the best story you ever heard. Today I'm just getting started in the Name of Jesus. The story takes place in the book of Matthew just to strengthen the listeners Matthew 11:28 repeat if you know it by heart. Come unto me, all ye that labor and are heavy laden, and I will give you rest.

Say with me Jesus never seeks the lime light or fame. Jesus living conditions from birth until his timely death was not comfortable. Jesus did it with a passion only God could provide during the birth of Jesus his family subdued all kinds of suffering you ever slept in a manger. Ask your neighbor have you ever slept in a manger not the Marriott, or Comfort Inn. A manger is only fit enough for a animal but it was just right for Jesus. Thank god for Jesus be grateful for your pillow-top mattress Amen.

Jesus Ministry didn't go to just the fancy places built by man the best places that is funny. Jesus didn't recruit the disciples in a genius contest all Jesus had to do ask his disciples were there Names-Birth Place-Do You Believe Jesus as you Lord and Savior. Jesus saves the lowly as well as high society So a man think so is HE. Jesus took his ministry to the cemetery, countryside, Leprosy territory, etc Places no one else would dare go with us Jesus went for you and me. When I was out in the world my mom and dad stopped chasing me. Jesus was right there with me.

(Matthew 11:29) Jesus said, "Take my yoke upon you, and learn of me; My mom and dad heard the word but they were not strong enough to allow the word to work they had to act on the those attitudes I had under their leadership. Jesus said For I am meek and lowly in heart: Jesus is the only one that already knows the outcome of all good or bad situations. Jesus is just right equally with all his children because he knew us before we were even created. And ye shall find rest unto your souls.

Jesus also says Foxes have their holes. Every bird their nests the son of God has no place to rest. Jesus is in every living creature resting in and outside everything breathing. Jesus performed miracles I am a living miracle of God's creation I believe Jesus died on the cross for us for all sins. Jesus didn't want to be seen Ego is not for Jesus people put on their fabric they could today. Just to get, "A you look nice huh look at some one and say you look nice Amen!! Over all (Matthew 11:30) confirms that Jesus is the way: For my yoke is easy, And my burden is light. Regardless of what you did good or bad Jesus still loves you Amen!!

2sweet

> I almost started crying when you were up there Mr. Sensitive Ha Ha!!!!

C-Luv

> What you talking about you sounded like you were preaching I heard you up there overwhelmed

2sweet

> We both know the word for the wages of sin is death; you know it as well as I do lately you haven't been yourself C-Luv

C-Luv

> But the gift of God is eternal life through Jesus Christ our Lord and Savior I know things have been difficult for me lately

2sweet

> Read this scripture (Act 4:12) Neither is there salvation in any other for there is none other name you know it

C-Luv

> Under Heaven given among men, whereby we must be saved

2sweet

Must be saved not kind of maybe Let us boast in the Lord C-Luv you no (James 4:17) we good say it are we good

C-Luv

Therefore to him that know to do good, and doeth not, to him is sin

2sweet

Amen! Therefore to him that know to do good, and doeth not, to him is sin

2sweet

Let not the wise man boast of his wisdom

C-Luv

Or the strong man, boast of his strength.

2sweet

Or the rich man, boast of his riches;

C-Luv

But him who boasts boast about this

2sweet

That he understands and knows Jesus,

C-Luv

That Jesus is the Lord, who works kindness, justice and righteousness on earth,

2sweet

For in these I delight

C-Luv

Hey man

2sweet

Say what you got to say spill it I can see that something is bothering you

Narrator

C-Luv thinking about the set-up
HUH Nothing it's a shame my life don't add up to the
word that good

2sweet

Don't beat yourself up it is progress not perfection

C-Luv

You have a nice time at church I got things to do
holla at you later

2sweet

If it be God's Will I will see you after while peace

Tucker's Church
JAX-MESSAGE ©

Tucker

I'm turning service over to the Sunshine Band at this
time.

Jax

Yes Jesus, "Say Yes," Praise the Lord.

Pristine

Thank you Jesus, Yes Lord.

Tucker

we have a business meeting to attend I know you
can handle it from here

Felicia

Don't get up there and start showing out either hear
me

Jax

Yes-Momma

Pristine

Yes-Momma

Tucker

We need about 15 minutes I'll be back thank you

Jax

First giving Honor to God who is the head of my life
I am nothing without God

Felicia

Take your time

Jax

Real quick give me ST. John 11:25

Felicia

Jesus said, unto her, "I am the resurrection, and the
life: he that believeth in me,
Though he were, yet shall he live.

Jax

And Matthew 11:26

Pristine

Good is good, And whosoever liveth and believeth
in me shall never die.

Jax

Believeth thou this?

Felicia

Amen you can do it!!

Pristine

You can do it I know you can

Jax

How many of us understand no one can become the
person God wants you to be
But through Jesus.

Members

        Amen Amen

Jax

        You got to go through Jesus to get to Heaven I will go even farther

Felicia

        Where you going don't go to far

Jax

        Even a Genius can be a ignorant at times

Pristine

        He's going home with it listen it's the good part I heard this one before

Jax

        Ignorant people may have high IQ's admirable reputations yet wise people view
Them as disasters.

Pristine

        Ignorant people ignore the wisdom God has to offer

J.B.

        Fools are crowd pleasers, and conceited folk.

Jax

        Ignorant people are the type of people who think themselves to be very clever

Travis

        Their cleverness lands them in trouble everytime

Trent

        No set of rules in a ignorant persons character can keep him or her out of trouble

Jax

> The bottom line for God's children today is:
> A wise person following God ought to recognize ignorance from far away and stay away from his or her path Amen!!

Pristine-Message ©

Jax

> I would like to welcome Ms-Pristine by giving her a hearty Amen!!

Pristine

> Praise the Lord, Praise the Lord Again it's truly a Honor to be here once again

Felicia

> Thank You Jesus

Pristine

> I feel like going on, I feel like going on

Jax

> Sing it sister Come On

Pristine

> How many of you out there feel like going on

Felicia

> Crying waving her hands telling other members they are so precious

Pristine

> I got to say it I just got to Matthew 11:28

Trent

> Amen, Praise the Lord, Praise the lord

Pristine

Come unto me, all ye that labour and are heavy laden, and I will give you rest.

Reggie

I don't know what you came to do but I came to praise the Lord.

Chauncey

I FEEL LIKE GOING ON, as the Lord will allow me.

Pristine

Right now Lord all I got is right now in the Name of Jesus

Kokomo

What she know about bringing a message

Pristine

I will be speaking today about Sin as a Cancer

Jax

I Know what my sister know about that Preach

Pristine

First David, then his Family, Then a Nation

Felicia

Amen

Pristine

God views Sins as Cancer not parking tickets read Matthew 11:29

Jax

Take my yoke upon you, and learn of me; for I am meek and lowly in heart: and
Shall find rest unto your souls

Trent

Obey the rules obey the rules

Pristine

I'm almost done in traffic the cops track you down

Felicia

Give your car the boot

Pristine

Huh If you get too many traffic tickets Amen

Reggie

Yes indeed

Pristine

Cancer makes a difference between life and death

Jax

Cancer grows, and multiplies

Chauncey

Taking over, major surgery is needed preach sister

Pristine

Many people need surgery to save their life, many people will see their well run dry also

Jax

Their lives will slip away we need to stay strong and pick up the pieces

Pristine

Just like David did Amen

Tucker

Amen Amen

Felicia

Wonderful message you two are a Blessing from God Thank You Jesus

Pristine

Jesus says For my yoke is easy, and my burden is light

Tucker

> We need to celebrate these two lovely young people preaching so powerful

Trent

> Let us say Amen for Jax and Pristine they sure did bring the message

Felicia

> I have been slacking to put it that way lately "Parking Tickets" Lord have mercy

Reggie

> But God is good all the time pray for me

(Church Sings)

J.B.

> I'm a soldier in the army of the Lord.

2sweet

> I wonder what was wrong with C-Luv It's just not like him to avoid me like that

Duke

> (Pumping his fist)

Man Man

> I thought I told you We soldiers mark.

2sweet

> I know times are hard for everybody C-Luv got to snap out of it some how

Duke

> We get it how we live out here you'll see

2sweet

>You two stoogers got stripes now all of a sudden you brave-hearted huh huh

Man Man

>This time we aint playing slap boxing homeboy

Duke

>Don't even think about running I see you looking for an outlet

2sweet

>I don't see know killers I'm looking for the rest of your help you gone need it

Man Man

>You always got jokes it's all fun and games until somebody get

Duke

>You feel me huh you feel me huh

2sweet

>You can have all the scams and plots off grams and rocks you're still stoogers

Duke

>Lay it down and shut up Mr. Tuff Guy

2sweet

>With Jesus I'm a Beast, a King, Make me shut up

Man Man

>Why you testing me huh

2sweet

>(Sizing up) Man Man/Duke

Duke

>You think you can handle this, You think you can handle this huh

2sweet

You couldn't fight your way out of a wet paper bag just lames

Duke

(Swinging) Yelling-We keeping it real, And missed

2sweet

I aint backing down Jesus won't let me (Moving)

Man Man

You a real stand up guy haha

Duke

It aint over yet!!!

2sweet

I deal with reality by seperating the fakes learned that along time ago Busters

Man Man

It aint over!!

2sweet

Knocks Duke/Man Man down and kicks Man Man in the stomach

Duke

On the ground yelling-You can't run forever

2sweet

Walking away saying-I'm down for mine on peaceful days and violent nights

Man Man

You can't run forever

2sweet

Do you two stoogers have any idea what Jesus life was like

Man Man

He got chips on his shoulders any of us could die tonight

Duke

We on top now

2sweet

(Where I Came From) Yall lucky I aint shoot like I use to do stoogers

Man Man

You got that same story same hood same old same it's all good

Duke

One day you gone slip up and we got you

2sweet

I got plenty of Space and opportunity to sweat the jabb on you two stoogers

Man Man

We gone catch you don't even trip

2sweet

Walking To Church

Elder Scott

Don't they know:
Neither is there salvation in any other:
For there is none other name under heaven given among men, whereby we must be saved.

2sweet

I can't believe them stoogers what's done gotten into them looney tunes

Elder Scott

Before we get started I would like to point out how good God is through Jesus

Bro Graves

Jesus handles tough situations and questions

Members

Amen!!!

Elder Scott

Now in (Daniel 6:10) When Daniel knew that the writing was signed, he went into his house;

2sweet

Reading-And his windows being open in his chamber toward Jerusalem, he kneeled upon his knees three times a day,

Bro Graves

And prayed, and gave thanks before his God, As he did aforetime

Elder Scott

(Verse-16) Look then the King Commanded, and they Brought Daniel, and cast him into the Den of Lions

2sweet

(Reading)-Now the King spake and said what huh what

Members

What did he say what did he say

Elder Scott

Huh What did he say now

2sweet

> Thy God who thou serve continually, he will deliver thee Amen

Elder Scott

> That is remarkable nerve to speak against God that way

Ma'June

> Daniel was untouched my God is Good all the time

Elder Scott

> The word never changes people change Jesus says in (Matt 11:28)
> Come unto me, all ye that labour not some but all, and are heavy laden, and I will give you rest. Read

Ma'Hampton

> Take my yoke upon you, and learn of me; for I am meek and lowly in heart: and ye shall find rest unto your souls

Elder Scott

> My message Today is teaching Jesus handling tough questions. Rumors buzzed about two Catastrophies.

Elder Scott

> Pontius Pilates slaughter of Galileans and the collapse of a tower

Members

> (Luke 13:1-4) Naturally people of the world questioned Jesus about these events,
> Jesus answers puzzled them. Jesus refuses to be drawn into a discussion of the age old problem of pain.

(Jesus merely discussed the common opinion that tragedies happen to people who deserve them and deflected the issue back to the questioners as a general warning.

You can see what Job (13:4-5) Job teaches about suffering. The heart of the question Jesus response to the questions on suffering illustrated how Jesus dealt with difficult issues.

Jesus is always conscious; of the listening crowds, Jesus avoided long arguments instead emphasizing the need for people to change behavior.

Jesus answers cut to the heart of the question, and to the hearts of his listeners!

(Ps-34:17-19)

Members

Doing what is good-(Titus 3:3-8)

Elder Scott

At one time or another we were all out there acting up say yes Amen or something We lived in malice and envy.

Being hated and hating one another. Jesus was hated and withstood the pressure and pain for us. Jesus was hated for being innocent and he still wept for those who did him wrong

Elder Scott

That's the kindness and love of God I am talking about praise Jesus when you all good, when you tempted when you broke angry happy or sad praise him

Elder Scott

Jesus died for us not because of our righteousness but because he is righteous. Jesus saves through the washing and rebirth and renewal by the Holy Spirit. Jesus poured out His generosity through Jesus Christ our Lord and Saviour being justified by his grace.

Elder Scott

We might become heirs having hope of eternal life
This is a trust worthy saying:
And I want you to stress these things so that you who have trusted in God maybe careful to devote themselves to doing what is good.
These things are excellent and profitable for everyone by Christ Jesus our Lord and Saviour

Act-2 of Play

Felicia

O God please Allow my family to seek you for help.

Counselor

Help us we need your Son Jesus our Savior to heal and cast out our trauma

Felicia

Let the Holy Ghost melt down the walls of suspicion and hostility we need you

Counselor

No matter how hard our lives maybe we could never suffer like you Jesus

Felicia

I feel like I'm living in a state of Quarantine I'm leaning on you O Lord, you will Not reject me, or forsake me.

Counselor

Strengthen our weaknesses build up our most Holy Faith in your will and way

Felicia

Yes Lord our faith in you God consider us O God when you send your deliverance for our dilemma

Counselor

Help the victims in these abusive relationships to conquer and overcome all the obstacles in healing

Felicia

I know I haven't been doing everything right O God have mercy on me you didn't bring me this far to leave me

Counselor

Keep us turn our lives around guide us to be more than conquerors in Jesus Name

Felicia

In the Name Of Jesus Make us whole again complete your will for us these are the prayers

Counselor

These are the prayers we ask in Jesus Name Thank God Thank God Amen

Narrator

Felicia/Counselor
One day all will be perfect again nothing can separate us from God's Love

Narrator

(John 11:25)

Jesus said unto her, I am the resurrection, and the life; he that believeth in me, though he were dead, yet shall he live:

Jax

Why does God Choose to use imperfect people like Jacob and us for examples (Humans)

Pristine

Yeah we need to know? We didn't ask to be here on earth it was part of God's design for us

Counselor

We have all had things happen to us in the past, present, and future.

Jax

Well in our case our parents love things happening so that makes them prime examples

Felicia

You would think we knew not to try and deceive God we are not perfect things just got out of control and instead of praying through the issues they grew worse

Counselor

Most people can't handle the results of the problems properly that's what makes matters worse

2sweet

Unless, Unless you are trying to improve your ways in Gods eyes it's useless

Pristine

There's no excuse you either do right or wrong no in
between no in between I thank God for Jesus

Jax

The Big picture is the love of Jesus people naturally
get caught-up in selfishness

Counselor

God always makes the choice, and God is always
right right

2sweet

The choice God makes doesn't depend on how
a person behaves to bring out the solution to a
problem

Jax

God simply chooses the people he wants plus
he places people in the situation to assist in the
process

Counselor

Just knowing all this information is true but has no
meaning if you do no t apply it to your lives

Pristine

We have no right finding fault with God's choices
God chose our parents we are here to discuss the
issues

2sweet

All of the rejected Brothers of (Genesis) were all
treated more than fairly in God's eyes

Felicia

Yeah, like wise in our situation God's judgment gets
the last say and who were those Brothers again

Jax

Cain, Canaan, Ishmael to name a few

Pristine

Don't leave out Reuben, Esau, and Manasseh yeah that's them

Felicia

That goes to show us not to question God's wisdom we may never understand God's choices no questioning God

Pristine

Unquestionably God's choices work for the good

Jax

The whole world becomes eligible to join the chosen people

Counselor

God chooses Flawed people to achieve good cause anyone can come to Christ Jesus

Jax

Yep Jesus came so that he could set us apart from the old way we as individuals use to behave to do the Will of His Father

Pristine

So who can say what God is doing with the hypocrites of our day or with my dad Tucker God be the judge

Narrator

The entire Group
Who can say what God is doing with the hypocrites of our day
Who can say

Counselor

Thank you for your time and patience in this therapy group session who you see here what you hear stays here

Jax

We will be sure to keep in touch with you never know when we may need you again

2sweet

Do you make house calls I think it's real good to vent in this room but at home is a different story all together we can't voice our opinion this open at home

Pristine

Yeah we can really let it all hang out at home so keep us in your prayers

Tucker Enters Church Loud

Tucker

Hey! What's Up

Man Man

Huh hey my dues are paid

Narrator

Duke

Makes head gesture hello laughing

Tucker

Man Man if your dues are paid what you talking for huh why do you have change for a penny

Narrator

Tucker in Man Man face

Tucker

> Huh Huh well be quiet Don't say nothing you need to think for a minute before you open your mouth

Narrator

> Felicia comes out of the sanctuary yelling

Felicia

> Tucker will you calm down we can hear you all the way in the sanctuary

Narrator

> Man Man Drinks water choking

Tucker

> What is so hilarious about losing money and the police questioning us can anyone answer that

Duke

> Is that all what's really going on here you are obviously upset with the wrong people

Narrator

> (L.B. drinks water)
> (Tucker snatches water from L.B. Tucker pours it on him)
> (Felicia hands L.B. a napkin)
> (Jax and Pristine Run Away)
> (Tucker yells at Felicia/L.B.)

Tucker

> Both of you get down there and wipe the water up now since you all so helpful

Man Man

> Well sorry about your situation you going through Tucker you need to calm down

Duke

> Clam down Tucker your children just ran out the door they running away I heard them run out the building you don't even care

Tucker

> Don't apologize clean this messy church up hear me

Duke

> You are seriously disturbed your children have just ran away for the thousandth time we in trouble everything is going hay-wire Tucker you need to calm down

Man Man

> For real you are so right regardless of what you going through Sir Jax and Pristine are gone that is important to me anyway

Tucker

> What you say to me What did you say to me What they ran off did you go after them or just watch them run

Narrator

> (Felicia crying down on the floor To God)

Felicia

> Dear God I can't take no more I can't take no more of this abuse from no man husband or not help me

L.B.

> Felicia you okay are you okay

Narrator

> (Felicia eyes closed praying)

L.B.

God you exactly what this situation calls for usher in the Holy Ghost Have you way refresh Sis. Felicia in the Name Of Jesus

Narrator

(Tucker tries to chase Jax/Pristine)

Tucker

Jax!! Pristine!! Come back here!!

Man Man

Tucker done lost his ever loving mind I got his number if he keep on disrespecting me

Duke

You heard all that foolishness he crazy running off at the mouth I know he upset but enough is enough

Man Man

You know it

Duke

He better know it

Man Man

Hurry up let's find 2sweet before Tucker become a victim

Narrator

Jax/Pristine run into 2sweet during the runaway

Jax

2sweet am I glad to see you we been running for at least a hour

Pristine

Yeah I'm not a track star I'm tired of running Jesus didn't run this much he fled

Jax

See Fled isn't running no one recorded ever seeing Jesus run he Fled into the crowd of people that's different

2sweet

Well I am sorry to rain on your parade but people have been shooting at me, I hate to say it but Run

Pristine

Are you serious told you we were already dysfunctional I told you

Jax

Will you come on now isn't the time to be fussing come on

2sweet

Can yall please run a little while longer come on please

Narrator

(2sweet Drag Pristine/Jax by the hands)

Pristine

Where are we going all my life never been in this neck of the woods

Jax

Good then we are safe cause Jesus died once and for all so we can live maybe you will listen to somebody shhh!

2sweet

Calm down all right, now we safe I can tell yall what I know

Pristine

Life really isn't a popularity contest

Jax

2sweet you living by the sword you gone die by it what going on cut to the chase

Pristine

Thank God I'm saved

Narrator

(Pristine Back-ground Singing He's Coming Back Again)

2sweet

I know hurting people hurt people and lately I haven't been running the streets for real

Jax

We have been getting lied to by mom/dad now you to Pristine found your stash the other day

Pristine

We up on your game now buddy word's kill people you don't have to sell poison to do it or carry a gun

2sweet

Sticks and stones huh are you two going to listen to me

Pristine

It's in God's hands any way 2sweet leave well enough alone

Jax

2sweet you put yourself in all these terrible situations now you want us to listen to you

Pristine

This better be great cause now you have involved us we in this together

Jax

Let's give 2sweet a break at least hear him out

Pristine

Make sure that you learn from this history in the making

Jax

Yeah or you will be doomed to continue to make the same mistakes so it has to be hard this time

Pristine

Does it hurt when we fall down yes we are ready to listen to you I think wait now

Jax

If we continue to keep running we will be running every time issues come up

2sweet

I can say this right now Thank God for his Son Jesus we need him right now first and foremost

Narrator

Jax/Pristine

Amen Amen

2sweet

We are here now so quiet down

Pristine

As long as we do not have to run no more

Jax

I'm not running no more okay 2sweet

Narrator

> (This entire time they were hiding in Eld. Scotts church)

Pristine

> Yeah 2sweet you don't have to convince us that people kill people

Jax

> Yeah the problem is people want to skip all the pain, and suffering and live forever

Pristine

> And Quote I say Bishop J.E. Patterson said, God stood on nothing and Spoke to nowhere

Jax

> Yep let there be and it was so that's power

Pristine

> 2sweet what's that thing on your shoulder's for the light on no one home (Hello)

Jax

> We are miracles created by God and only he can save us

Pristine

> Why are you in a gang any way you scared you need some protection ooow

Jax

> Yeah you feel tough running with your homies where they at now tough guy they probably the ones shooting at you

Pristine

> No matter how big you feel you only as big as your fist 2sweet

2sweet

> Well we here thanks for the sound advice you two I really wish I could explain but you will be cool now

Jax

> Change them people places and things you are doing to go against God and you will be alright

2sweet

> You two have been saying enough now we in church hush I know the streets are corrupt I'm trying

Pristine

> 2sweet why don't you join our gang

Jax

> What gang girl

Pristine

> That's right God gave it to me the other day for leadership

Jax

> Jesus lifestyle for us is in accordance to the word not no sign unless the word says it

Pristine

> Close your fists you listening (Jesus loves the little Children)

Jax

> Thank You Jesus I don't know what to say about that girl

Pristine

> Now both of you with your fists closed say knuckleheads for Jesus because when God calls us home we want to hear well done

(Mo. Hampton Looking Through purse fussing)

Mo. Hampton

Where is my grocery list I know I had it in this purse here it is Lord know I can't go to the store without it

Mo. June

You got to make those sweet potato pies now don't forget

Mo. Hampton

Them pies are already finished I'm really getting things my family forget to bring you know

Mo. June

Oh do I know they will come with the biggest appetite you ever saw ask the family to bring a dish or other things you got to beat them up

Mo. Hampton

You know I mentioned this year was going to be different everyone would have to pitch in well the guest list got short at my house

Mo. June

Family think cause you church going you will accept anything no it don't work that way

Mo. Hampton

Please I almost had to call the police you know I'm just playing but I didn't cook one day I was the only one at the house

Mo. June

What they do just unruly huh

Mo. Hampton

> Yeah asked me what was for dinner I said poke in grits

Mo. June

> Poke in Grits

Mo. Hampton

> Yeah poke out your mouth and grit your teeth

Mo. June

> All now Mo. Hampton it's a wonder they didn't cut you I never heard that one

Mo. Hampton

> I laughed so hard I got a head ache watching them sit around with all that good left-over food in that kitchen

Mo. June

> Young people just plain out don't know how to cook microwave this and that

Mo. Hampton

> What they gone do when we gone they can't boil eggs for salad right

Mo. June

> My family spent too much time and money all week long at the fast food restaurant

Mo. Hampton

> My great grand children eat sugar all day long bouncing off the walls before they get to my house

Mo. June

> Soon as they drop them off and I tell them great grand to sit down they have a fit I don't count to nothing switch

Mo. Hampton

O lord yes running all over furniture I tapped they behind one good time at my house they sat down until the next day

Narrator

(Mo. Hampton/Mo. June Laughing at the great grand behavior)

Mo. June

The children were so quiet when they got picked up somebody said I don't know what you did but keep doing it

Mo. Hampton

I told one of them great grand to go get a switch he bought the light fixture out of the garage to me

Narrator

(Mo. Hampton/Mo. June leaving grocery store)

Mo. June

Take it easy God Bless you

Mo. Hampton

Okay be safe God Bless

Narrator

(Man Man/ Duke rush in the store)

Man Man

There go Mo. Hampton Right Right Huuh!

Narrator

(Duke turning around looking)

Duke

>Where is she I don't see her where oooh! There she goo!!

Man Man

>Hey Mo. Hampton how are you doing today you look great

Duke

>Oh Hey Mo. Hampton there go that smile you so sweet Mother

Man Man

>I was just thinking about you earlier sure was

Duke

>How your family doing I pray everyone is fine Mo. Hampton

Mo. Hampton

>How are you young men doing miss you at church we really miss you young men

Man Man

>We need to come more often to hear the word it has been a while

Duke

>Really it has I can't even say I be too busy either I really don't be up to much just lazy

Narrator

>(Man Man Elbows Duke)

Man Man

>Well there's church service tonight isn't it Mo. Hampton

Mo. Hampton

> Yeah there sure is you need a ride your welcome to ride to church with me I can have someone pick yall up

Man Man

> You sure Mo. Hampton we can ride with you if it's not too much

Duke

> We really appreciate it

Narrator

> (Man Man/Duke whisper)
> Yeah 2sweet better be at church tonight
> Yeah he better be there
>
> (Felicia down on the floor crying loud)

Felicia

> Wonderful Saviour I need your strength and deliverance bless us with your keeping power we need to be kept in the wonderful name of Jesus

Det. Reggie

> Come on in Lord yea, Lord Come in Lord we need you abide in your children we crying out to you Glory to God

Felicia

> My mind is made up I give my whole heart and soul to you my soul says yes to your Will I am sick and tired of all this pity and vengeance help me right now yes Jesus

Det. Reggie

> We need your yes Jesus Jesus Jesus change our situations from dark to light uplift your spirit in your children Jesus Jesus O Jesus

Trent

> Bless each and everyone right now Jesus you know our needs your know our troubles lead and guide us Jesus

Det. Reggie

> You'll never leave us nor forsake us you stand at the door and hear our cry come on in Jesus

Felicia

> Forgive me Forgive me Forgive us Jesus you're my everything I am not ashamed of you Jesus

Det. Reggie

> Save us from ourselves Jesus O Jesus Lead us beside the still waters restore our souls Jesus

Trent

> We plead The Blood of Jesus Jesus protect our soul hearts and minds we want to do right by you Jesus

Felicia

> I don't live scorned and battered any longer help me Jesus I need you more Jesus

Det. Reggie

> Heal our illnesses take away our addictions wipe away our problems let us come to you o Jesus

Trent

> Let peace abide in our Homes at work in the Church Jesus we need you everywhere we go in the quiet

moments in the loud times help all of us in the name of Jesus

Felicia

Jesus Jesus Jesus my soul says yes to your Will yes to your way

Det. Reggie

We living witnesses of your glory worship a living God in our belly shall flow rivers of living water. Yes to your Will and Way Jesus Jesus!!

Felicia

I believe I can't do this by my will Thy Will be done remove the trauma from my life yes Jesus

Trent

The world didn't give and the world can't take it away we have a right to worship and praise you Jesus

Det. Reggie

You are in control Jesus yes Jesus Jesus

Felicia

Jesus Thank You Jesus Jesus heal the sick strengthen our health thank you for today

Det. Reggie

I am nothing without you Jesus Jesus

Felicia

I will not put nothing before you Jesus I don't want to be abused again Jesus

Trent

Send your deliverance Jesus in the name of Jesus Satan the Lord rebuke you in the name of Jesus

Det. Reggie

You know the way Jesus allow us to stay focused on you Jesus

Felicia

I am no good to you or my family in the grave I need you Jesus

Narrator

(All Members Together Pray)
These are the prayers that we ask in Jesus Name Thank God Amen Amen!!
Thank you Jesus Thank You Jesus

Felicia

At this time Service is open to all the people gathered together to enjoy the celebration of Jesus today so sing if you can, shout testify as unto the Lord about how great and worthy he is to be praised

C-Luv

I can't take it know more God, I need your strength to see me through this treacherous time

Det. Leslie

Sure it will be tough but don't be so hard on yourself this situation you are faced with will only make you stronger

C-Luv

The time is for me to trust in the Lord with all my heart, soul, and mind not leaning to my own understanding

Det. Leslie

I am truly sorry to hear about your parents are you all right

C-Luv

After the letter I received from those two I will not visit them ever again it's bad enough they became snitches

Det. Leslie

Your parents did their best without involving you in their mess

C-Luv

They were snitches all this time acting like they had it going on please

Det. Leslie

What is this gossip I hear about people trying to harm 2sweet he is your friend by the way

C-Luv

2sweet is alright it's Tucker who needs help Tucker hired Man Man/Duke to kill 2sweet before the New Members Program

Det. Leslie

What no wonder!! Oh Lord no this is gone too far

C-Luv

Tucker thought I would be stupid enough to work with them busters but I turned the offer down

Det. Leslie

Clam down calm down let us think through this situation looking for positive choices

C-Luv

> To be honest Man Man/Duke were the two cowards that set my mom and dad up on the murder of Mrs. Scott

Det. Leslie

> Do you mean that drive-by Allow the police handle it you just continue to do the next right thing please

C-Luv

> The cops have always been welcome in my life ask my parents Det. Leslie does it look like I'm playing Huh!!

Det. Leslie

> Remember you promised that you wouldn't do anything irrational if you take matters into your own hands now the law will not be on your side like we are right now

C-Luv

> Like Mom/Dad I can't believe this I am a snitch to there is no getting around this snitching when really it's just telling the truth

Det. Leslie

> C-Luv God has allowed you the opportunity to be corrupt for a long time you keep on ignoring his call to get right it may be too late

C-Luv

> My parents opened the door to my demise Tucker is in the way I'm about supply and demand I keep the circuit clean like a washing machine

Det. Leslie

> Allow the law to help you we can help you unlike your parents they need help also don't take the law into your own hands

C-Luv

> You need to catch them busters I'm telling it like it is catch them I hear you loud and clear the jokes will be all over if they run into 2sweet

Det. Leslie

> I will do everything in my power to find 2sweet first okay just be calm and stay out of trouble

C-Luv

> You got jokes here lately trouble has been finding me I haven't been out doing nothing guess it's from the bad seed I have sown

Det. Leslie

> Do you know anything else that would help me right now I need that information C-Luv

C-Luv

> I spilled my heart out to you Det. You still don't believe me that's all

C-Luv

> Heeey!!! Hey!!! There go Tucker right there

Det. Leslie

> Hey! Hey! Hey! C-Luv you are upset right now that still doesn't give you the right to put your hands on anybody

C-Luv

> But But wooooo!!! Man you really got some nerves

Narrator

(C-Luv stomping around gesturing like he wants to fight)

C-Luv

Tucker you got some nerves do you actually think you are untouchable do you

Tucker

Do something then bust a move C-Luv what you want from me

C-Luv

I want the truth as well as everyone else the truth about the murder of Mrs. Scott the truth about trying to kill never mind

Det. Leslie

C-Luv I just told you we will help you catch Man Man/Duke to find out the truth

C-Luv

My parents are not murderers they are taking the wrap for his stupidity I may as well take the law into my own hands

Tucker

Since you are so smart find out who killed my parents Ha! Ha! Ha!

C-Luv

Yall can't Arrest him we all know he's a Domestic Violence King, a petty hustler man just pitiful arrest him

Eld. Scott

Tucker you out here laughing playing all tough when is enough enough

Det. Leslie

> Tucker it's never to later to get help you have to sincerely want help

C-Luv

> What does it take to get arrested around here I been minding my own business here you come bothering me Arrest Him Arrest Him before someone else comes up missing because of his selfishness

Det. Leslie

> Yeah Tucker in order for the Dept. to help you we need serious vital information to these cases to help us work in your behalf

Eld. Scott

> Out of all the people I have seen murdered in cold blood (My Wife) she was one of those people I miss her all the time

Tucker

> we have all suffered looses in our lives family and friends what are you trying to say to me homeboy

C-Luv

> Tucker to think all this time I use to be jealous of 2sweet for having the family structure I wished for look at how you are acting (Please)

Det. Leslie

> I haven't saw my son in 27 years personally I worry about him every day I still can't come to work and take it out on innocent people

Eld. Scott

The lifestyle you choose to live reflects on your family it is our responsibility to be accountable for our actions good or bad

Narrator

(Tucker Kneeled on the ground crying)

Tucker

I lost it my family doesn't depend on me any more Oh Lord have Mercy on me

C-Luv

Dear God we are standing in need of healing power from the Holy Ghost lead and guide us protect us Bless those that haven't seen their children in years

Narrator

(Eld. Scott Steps to the side smiles as C-Luv pray closing his eyes)

Eld. Scott

Jesus Jesus you know my heart since my wife died my children abandoned our family bring them back to you place you love on their hearts soul and mind

Det. Leslie

We are not perfect forgive us for all our mistakes Jesus Yes Jesus strengthen our weakness we need you more than ever today

Eld. Scott

My children are in the hands of God lead and guide them save Lord save them protect them you know what is best for them heal Yes Jesus

C-Luv

> Jesus loves us regardless of our past present or future

Tucker

> Forgive me Heavenly father you know what is best for me from beginning to end

Eld. Scott

> As your son Saul cried out Lord Lord on the road to Damascus he could see but was spiritually blind Jesus opened up his eyes the more Yes Jesus

Det. Leslie

> Have mercy on your children help us take back what the devil stole from us in the Name of Jesus

Tucker

> I once was lost now I am found so that I can live life more abundantly and free

C-Luv

> Thank You Jesus for everything you have done and all that you already have taken care of for us

Det. Leslie

> All things will become new through Christ Jesus we Honor God as the head of our lives

Eld. Scott

> God loved my wife more than I did losing her life opened up my eyes t a new way of living had not I been running the streets she would have been safe

C-Luv

> God kept you alive so you could tell somebody

Det. Leslie

> The Police Dept. does not have any charges pending against you so therefore Tucker I can't place you in jail

Eld. Scott

> The Lord is on your side regardless of your wrong doing

Tucker

> I will be admitting myself into a (Rehab) Pray that God strengthens my weaknesses building my faith to do right

Narrator

> (Det. Leslie taking Tucker to the rehab)

Eld. Scott

> Hold fast to the word of God Thy will be Done in the Name Of Jesus

C-Luv

> Det. Leslie don't forget to give my parents that letter matter of fact let Tucker read it to them

Det. Leslie

> Lets Find Man Man/Duke before we have more uncalled for problems

Eld. Scott

> Calls for Sunshine band speeches (3)

The Choir

> The Choir Sing (2-Selections)

Eld. Scott

> Preach the Message: Jesus heals the blind man from birth

Narrator

      Eld. Scott

Alter call

Narrator

      (2sweet on the altar arms stretched out facing the pulpit)

Narrator

      (2sweet never turns around he's praying)

Narrator

      (Mo. Hampton runs in screaming C-Luv is dead Oh Lord)

Mo. Hampton

      It was a accident I didn't mean to run him over I just didn't see him help me Oh Lord

Narrator

      (Bro. Graves at the entrance of the sanctuary holding Man Man/Duke back)

      (Man Man/Duke road to the church with Mo. Hampton to hurt 2sweet)

Bro. Graves

      Get Back Get Back I can't allow you two gentlemen the opportunity to go in the church at all Get Back

Narrator

      Man Man/Duke trying to run in the sanctuary

Man-Man

      Move move out of the way

Narrator

(Man-Man) pushing and shoving trying to get around (Bro. Graves)

Duke

I going to get you 2sweet watch and see

Bro Matthews

Put them in the lobby I just got off the phone with Det. Leslie they are on their way to pick them up

Narrator

Man Man/Duke-Yelling

2sweet you buster you buster

Narrator

(Eld. Scott ignores the trouble going on in the lobby)

Eld. Scott

2sweet, Jax, And Pristine this is your precious moment before God ask him what you will and He will fix it

Det. Leslie

Please escort Mo. Hampton down to the station so we can take her statement about the accident

Narrator

Det. Reggie

Arrests Man Man/Duke as they talk stuff

Narrator

(Man Man) (It was all Tuckers idea he hired us that is the truth)

Trent

> We need every one to come back into the sanctuary please settle down now back to the reason we are here Jesus

Eld. Scott

> Before we go anywhere we enjoy having your family here in our presence hey 2sweet you are no longer a visitor we appreciate you coming out to services

Eld. Scott

> I just want to give you all a few scriptures to study up on for your selves Matt 11:28-30 Acts 4:12 John 11:25 Rom 6:23 james 4:17

Eld. Scott

> Come on choir take us out with 2 more selections something new may God Bless you all and Good night

Narrator

> Alter-Call
> > The Final Call-McGee Temple

Theme Song

> Turn Your Life Around-(cast/crew)

The End
God Bless You!!!

Nika this is it the entire manuscript I have had an experience of a lifetime dealing with this publishing. I am new to this but here goes a multi-million dollar project they said think big. This is all based on a true story I am happy to be a part of the team peace!